High Horses

'Brood mare, two foals and a filly',
a frieze painted by George Stubbs
for the Marquis of Rockingham

*Illustrated by Peter Gregory
and with prints and photographs*

Grant Uden

High Horses

Kestrel Books

Kestrel Books
Published by Penguin Books Ltd
Harmondsworth, Middlesex, England

Copyright © 1976 by Grant Uden
Illustrations Copyright © 1976 by Peter Gregory

First published 1976

ISBN 0 7226 5369 7

Filmset in Ireland by Doyle Photosetting Ltd, Tullamore
Printed in Great Britain by
Lowe & Brydone (Printers) Ltd., Thetford, Norfolk

Contents

The King's high horses
Came pacing one by one
With crinet and flanchard
Gleaming in the sun;
And, ugly as a griffon,
Came, too, the little hack,
Feet light and eye bright,
The pedlar on his back.
– The Pedlar of Puriton

Acknowledgements

The author and publisher wish to thank the following for permission to reproduce illustrative material in this volume: Aerofilms Ltd for page 76; The British Library Board for pages 89, 122 and 147; page 34, by permission of the Duke of Wellington photograph; Courtauld Institute; Culver Pictures for page 139; Fores Ltd for pages 61 and 134; The Hall of Fame of The Trotter for page 144 *above*; page 55 reproduced by kind permission of the Stewards of the Jockey Club; Keystone Press Agency for pages 74, 144 and 150; The Mansell Collection for pages 16, 30, 48, 62, 72, 118, 121, 129 *above*, 130, 137, 143, 146 *right*, 156 and 157; Radio Times Hulton Picture Library for pages 86, 112, 116 *left*, 120, 132 *below*, 135, 136, 138, 140, 146 *left*, 149 *above*, 149 *below* and 152; The Smithsonian Institution for page 133; Spink and Son Ltd for page 145; The Tate Gallery for page 155 *above*; pages 66, 124, 128, 142 and 151 are by courtesy of Arthur Ackerman and Son Ltd; 'Cypron and her brood' on page 127 is reproduced by gracious permission of Her Majesty the Queen.

The photo of William Holt and Trigger, page 154, is from *Trigger In Europe* by William Holt and is by courtesy of the author; Wandle Robert, page 155, is by courtesy of Young & Co. Brewery Ltd; Traveller, page 154, is by courtesy of National Park Service, USA; the cartoon on page 116 is from the *Punch* collection, *Pictures of Life and Character*, by John Leech; the painting of Arkle, page 74, is from *Between the Flags* by S. J. Watson, Allen Figgs Dublin, 1969; the Percheron cart stallion page 80, engraved by R. C. West, is from *The Book of the Horse* by S. Sidney, Cassell & Co., 1881; the Clydesdale stallion, Shire and Suffolk mares are from *The Points of the Horse* by M. Horace Hayes, Hurst & Blackett; the frontispiece is from *George Stubbs and Ben Marshall* by Walter Shaw Sparrow, Cassell & Co., 1929, the collection of Lord Fitzwilliam; 'Mr Wildman and his sons with Eclipse', page 129, is from the painting in Mr Walter Raphael's collection, reproduced in *George Stubbs and Ben Marshall*, Cassell & Co., 1929; Man O'War, page 141, is from *Racing in America 1866–1921* by W. S. Vosburgh, The Jockey Club, New York, 1922.

Foreword

We shall never know who first measured the height of his horse by the width of his hand. 'Hands' was already a standard measure in the reign of Henry VIII and must have been in use long before; a part of the homely system of calculation established by men who had no official weights and measures department and therefore used rough-and-ready familiar things – the length of a furrow in the ploughed field (the 'furrow long' or furlong), the maximum flight of an arrow, the distance a hen could fly, the amount of corn that could be passed through a crooked arm, the span between the spread little finger and thumb, the distance from the nose-end to the limit of an outstretched arm.

As part of this system it became customary to state the height of a horse in hands, or the width of a broad palm, later standardized at four inches and used to measure up the fore-leg to the withers, or ridge between the shoulder-blades. The measurement can be applied to anything from a tiny pony, standing three feet (9 hands) or less, to a giant Percheron or Shire draught horse towering up to six feet (18 hands).

But horses can be high in other things than inches – high in breeding, in spirit and courage, in fidelity, in performance, in strength and endurance, in the affection of their owners. They have played such a part in the affairs of man that the whole of human history would have been different without them. Indeed, much of the work of the world as we know it would have been impossible.

Only a few of their names and stories have survived and, perhaps inevitably, most of the best known are associated either with famous

9

soldiers or with the racecourse. But, along with them, should be re-membered the countless other high horses through the centuries –
those of the doctor, the courier, the farmer, the carrier, the merchant,
the pilgrim and the priest; the stage-horse, the pit pony, the dray-horse and the pack-horse – 'knowing nothing of the cause ... filled
only with faith, love, and loyalty'.

The Horse in War

After God, we owed the victory to the horses.
–Records of the Conquistadores, *c.* 1525

Introduction

It is strange to remember that, until little more than fifty years ago, the famous words of the Bible on the war-horse still had meaning on the battle-fields of Europe:

He saith among the trumpets, Ha, ha; and he smelleth the battle afar off, the thunder of the captains and the shouting.

The Book of Job, from which the quotation comes, was probably written in the fourth century B.C.; and in St Jude's Church, Hampstead, north-west London, is a memorial recording that 375,000 horses fell on the British side in the Great War of 1914–18.

The horse is one of the earliest symbols in history of kingship, power and military might. On coins and ancient pottery, in sculpture, mosaics, paintings and illuminations, the warriors ride high, with their vassals and servants beneath them. The finest horses were bred for battle and tournament, daintier but less strong mounts often being used in procession and parade.

It is understandable that many soldiers and famous knights are associated with particular horses, either as a matter of historical fact or through folk-lore and legend. Thus, the outlaw Hereward the Wake, celebrated for his fight against William the Conqueror, had his mare Swallow; the Castilian hero Rodrigo, Diaz de Bivar ('Cid Campeador' or 'the lord champion'), had his Babieca (meaning 'simpleton'); the Chevalier Bayard, the knight 'sans peur et sans reproche', rode a fine Persian called Carman; the English Earl of Warwick, 'the Kingmaker', went into battle on Black Saladin. George Washington had two favourite horses, one a splendid chestnut which he rode on parade; the other a much less elegant sorrel which he called for when action was imminent, so that, when the troops saw the general on the sorrel, they said 'We have business in hand.'

I

Ox-Head

c. 356–326 B.C.

Alexander, king of Macedon, who died in the year 323 B.C. at the age of thirty-three, is perhaps the shortest-lived ruler in history on whom the title 'the Great' has been bestowed without any question of its rightness. The son of Philip of Macedon, he came to the throne at the age of twenty and in the next few years decisively defeated the mighty Persian armies, conquered Egypt and overran large areas in India. He is described as having been of medium height, with his head carried somewhat aslant, and his hair standing over his forehead like a lion's. His clean-shaven face set a long-lasting fashion in the ancient civilized world.

Opinion among historians is divided about the truth of his greatness. It is beyond dispute that he had great courage and energy; but it will always be a matter for argument whether he was a ruler of true vision, enlightenment and mercy, or a man of crazy ambition and vainglory who, according to the story, wept because there were no more worlds to conquer.

If the account given by the Greek historian Plutarch, writing some four and a half centuries after Alexander's death, is true, as a young prince the future conqueror showed a shrewd intelligence and powers of observation.

Alexander's father, King Philip, had been offered a horse named Bucephalus by Philonicus, a merchant from North Greece. The price demanded was high and seemed to indicate an animal of unusual worth and character. But when the king, attended by his nobles, went into the fields to see the horse show his paces, they found a vicious and unmanageable beast who would not allow himself to be mounted and who lashed out vindictively at his grooms.

Philip was angry that such an evil-tempered horse should have been offered him and ordered that he should be taken away; but he was surprised to hear the voice of the young Prince Alexander say:

'What a horse they are losing, for want of skill and spirit to manage him!'

At first the king took no notice, but when Alexander repeated it, he said sharply:

'My lad, you find fault with your elders as if you know better than they and could manage the horse better.'

Alexander apparently stood in no fear of his powerful father, for he answered boldly enough:

'I certainly could.'

The king studied him a moment, then said:

'And if I allow you to try and you should fail, what forfeit will you pay?'

'I myself will pay the price of the horse to Philonicus.'

Bronze statue of Alexander taming
Bucephalus

The company of courtiers enjoyed this exchange, with its note of harsh seriousness beneath light-hearted words, and there was general laughter. King Philip shrugged and agreed to the bargain, then watched, not without some nervousness, as the young prince ran to where the spirited horse was still defiantly holding his grooms at bay. It seems that Alexander, watching closely the previous attempts to ride him, had noticed something that had escaped the other onlookers.

The rest of the story is told in Plutarch's words, as translated by two scholars, John and William Langhorne, in 1831:

Alexander ran to the horse, and laying hold of the bridle, turned him to the sun; for he had observed, it seems, that the shadow which fell before the horse, and continually moved as he moved, greatly disturbed him. While his fierceness and fury lasted, he kept speaking to him softly and stroking him; after which he gently let fall his mantle, leaped lightly upon his back, and got his seat very safe. Then, without pulling the reins too hard, or using either whip or spur, he set him a-going. As soon as he perceived his uneasiness abated, he put him in a full gallop and pushed him on both with the voice and spur.

Philip and all his court were in great distress for him at first, and a profound silence took place. But when the prince had turned him and brought him straight back, they all received him with loud acclamations, except his father, who wept for joy, and, kissing him, said: 'Seek another kingdom, my son, that may be worthy of thy abilities; for Macedonia is too small for thee.'

Thus Alexander acquired his favourite charger, black with a white blaze on his forehead, and named Bucephalus, or 'Ox-Head'. Perhaps the name was given because of the shape of the blaze or from a particular brand on the shoulder. The purchase price of thirteen talents has been worked out at over £5000 in modern currency.

Alexander never had cause to regret the bargain. Bucephalus carried him in most of his triumphant campaigns, never losing his fierce pride and the spirit that had been his as a colt. Nevertheless, he was so well trained that, when arrayed for procession or battle, he would kneel before his master, waiting for him to mount.

Many legends and stories arose about Bucephalus. It is told, for example, that a famous artist named Appeles painted a portrait of the splendid young conqueror and his horse. Alexander did not seem particularly impressed with the work, but it was so lifelike that Bucephalus neighed in greeting. The artist turned to the Emperor and said: 'Your majesty's horse is a better judge of a painting than his noble master.'

It seems fairly certain that the horse lived till about 326 B.C. and died at the age of thirty or more, either in battle in India or of old age and weariness after his strenuous career. Plutarch tells us:

Alexander showed as much regret as if he had lost a faithful friend and companion. He esteemed him, indeed, as such; and built a city near the Hydaspes, in the place where he was buried, which he called, after him, Bucephalus.

In the Punjab district of India is the modern town of Jhelum or Jhelam on the bank of the river of the same name, and near by is an ancient mound which archaeologists have identified as the site of Alexander's city of Bucephalus.

About 1600 years after these events, a young merchant of noble family in Venice named Marco Polo travelled right across Asia to the court of the great ruler Kublai Khan, whose empire extended from the China Sea to the Black Sea. Marco compiled the first European account of Asia, and of the kingdom of Balashan (or Badaskshan) he wrote:

The horses bred there are of a superior quality and have great speed. Their hoofs are so hard that they do not require shoeing. The natives are in the practice of galloping them on declivities where other cattle could not or would not venture to run. They asserted that not long since there were still found in this province horses of the breed of Alexander's celebrated Bucephalus, which were all foaled with a particular mark in the forehead.

This may well have been the blaze of the ox-head.

2
Saladin's Gift

A.D. 1192

We do not know the names of the horses involved in the incident described here, though they will be remembered as long as tales of knighthood and chivalry are told and read. Each was undoubtedly a true *Sh'rubah Er'rech* or 'wind drinker' of the type described 700 years later as 'of great muscular development; sinews clean and hard as pinwire ... fair and square on the best of limbs and joints. High-couraged, bold, free, clever as a cat ...' This owner could not find enough adjectives to describe his Arabian.

The incident happened in 1192 when Richard I, before he left the Holy Land a disappointed and dispirited man, won his last and most spectacular victory against the Saracens, led by the redoubtable Salah ad-Din Yusaf, known more simply to later generations as Saladin. Rarely have two opposing leaders, of equal courage and ruthlessness in battle, been so unlike.

Richard was 'lofty of stature, of shapely build, his hair halfway between red and yellow, his limbs straight and supple. His arms were somewhat long and, therefore, better fitted than of most folk to draw or wield a sword. He had, moreover, long legs in keeping with the character of his whole frame.' Saladin was slight of build. His face 'melancholy in repose ... would readily light up with a charming smile.' He was a modest man of simple tastes in contrast with his towering, exuberant, show-loving opponent.

But if they were unlike in physical appearance and disposition, they shared at least two sentiments – respect for each other and admiration for courage.

In July 1192 Saladin had descended on the important port of

Jaffa and taken it after a three-day siege. Richard was in Acre when they brought him the news. Hardly pausing to make battle plans, Coeur de Lion summoned his captains and sent his army on a forced march overland. With the rest of his knights he took ship and stood into the port of Jaffa, at the head of fifty galleys. Scarcely had the first keels grated when the king was in the water, splashing ashore with the sea flecking his mail. Eighty knights hurled themselves against the citadel, backed up by some 400 archers and 2000 other troops. The knights could muster only three horses among them. It was a small enough force, but it was enough. The defeated Christian garrison inside the walls took arms again and joined in the battle. Soon Jaffa was retaken and the victorious crusaders camped beneath the walls, awaiting the arrival of their supporting army, coming overland.

Saladin reassembled his men and determined to smash Richard before the reinforcements could arrive. Seven formidable waves of Saracen cavalry, each a thousand strong, swept on the Christian camp, one after the other. At first Richard fought standing still, his men in pairs behind a shield wall, their spears stuck in the ground with the points angled outwards. Charge after charge thundered down and broke. Time after time the Moslems wheeled, galloped away, reformed and attacked again.

As the momentum slackened and the horses began to flag, Richard, calculating the situation to a nicety, gave new orders. His archers took up the battle, advancing to the front and sending their flights of yard-long arrows straight into the ranks of oncoming horsemen before stepping back again behind the shield wall. Then, as the Saracens faltered, Richard himself came roaring into the fight at the head of his tiny company of horsemen.

This was the Richard the Saracens were to remember long after the English king had left Palestine, the warrior seemingly almost superhuman in strength, clearing a swathe around him, his yellow hair beneath the battle-helm bright amidst the swarthy faces of his enemies.

The surest way to bring down a knight was to attack his horse, and soon Richard was on the ground. But almost at once, feet free of the twisting stirrups, he was on his feet, battling on in the thick of the rearing Saracen horses, his knights and his enemies in dust-wrapped confusion around him.

Then a strange thing happened. Pressing through the struggling warriors came a soldier leading two snorting horses, fresh for the fight.

Fresh horses . . . not for some Saracen emir whose mount was worn out from hours of battle, but for the Christian king; horses not from the English ranks, but sent as a gift to Richard of England from Salah ad-Din Yusaf Ibn Eyub, Sultan of Egypt and Syria, in tribute from one brave man to another.

Long after he left the Holy Land, the legend of Richard lived on. Jean, Sire of Joinville, tells us in his Memoirs of the Crusades, completed in about A.D. 1309:

> When the Saracen children cried, their mothers called out: 'Whisht! here is King Richard!' in order to keep them quiet. And when the horses of the Saracens and Bedouins started at a tree or bush, their masters said to the horses: 'Do you think that is King Richard?'

3
The Black God

c. A.D. 1525

Yucatan is a peninsula of central America, separating the Gulf of Mexico and the Caribbean Sea. Its earliest inhabitants were Indians known as Maya, a dark-skinned, short and sturdy people whose descendants still form the greater part of the inhabitants of modern Yucatan. The Maya had a highly developed civilization which flourished from about the fourth to the eighth century and which continued to rise and fall till they were finally conquered by the Spaniards in the sixteenth century.

The Maya were skilful in pottery and painting, they devised a calendar and a system of handwriting, they reared great stone temples decorated with sculptures and raised high on stepped pyramids dominating the countryside. Probably the temples acted also as observatories, for much of the Maya religion was connected with the observation of sun, moon and stars. But amid all their elaborate art and sculpture there is no record of the horse, either as a beast of burden or as appropriate transport for their princes and nobles.

It is, in fact, one of the mysteries of history that, for a long period, the horse seems to have disappeared from both North and South America. Judging from the many fossils found, horses crossed from Asia in the distant ages when a land bridge with that continent still existed, and they seem to have survived the glacial period, when ice covered much of the earth, only to be completely wiped out later, perhaps by some acute disease.

The ancient Maya deities included Itzamna, the sky god; Kukulkan, the creator god, who presided over the calendar, arts and crafts; and the gods of rain, maize, the sun and the planet Venus. Kukulkan,

too holy and remote to be represented in human form, appears as a feathered serpent, a combination of snake and the resplendent quetzal bird.

In the sixteenth century, some of the Indians descended from the ancient Maya acquired a mysterious new object of worship, a curious type of seated horse which became in time one of the most potent gods of all, expressing his power in the terror of the storms rumbling round the high plateaus, flashing on the crumbling temples and deserted cities of their ancestors.

Hernan Cortés, Marquis of Oaxaca and former Governor of Mexico, might have been surprised had he heard of it, but not displeased; for it was surely proper that the Indians should show due reverence to the horse of a Spanish conquistador. Cortés, greatest of the generals who conquered Mexico, later fell out of favour with his emperor, Charles V, and, it is related, once forced his way through the crowd surrounding the emperor's carriage and mounted the step. When asked who he was he replied: 'I am a man who has given you more provinces than your ancestors left you cities.'

Cortés was thirty-four years old when, in 1519, he landed in Mexico with ten ships, some eighteen horses, 600 foot soldiers and a small body of artillery. To the Indians it was an awe-inspiring sight – especially the steel-clad figures on their horses. It is not surprising that the Spaniards were looked upon as gods and that Cortés, with the sun gleaming on helmet, back and breastplate, was hailed as a descendant of the sun itself.

One of his companions described him as 'a gallant and courageous captain ... affable in his manner and a good talker ... He cared nothing for silks and damask, nor did he wear heavy gold chains but just a thin chain of gold of a simple pattern.' This friend, Bernal Diaz del Castillo, also recorded that Cortés was somewhat bow-legged and a very good horseman, skilful with all weapons mounted or on foot.

In 1524 Cortés was in Yucatan pushing southward to Honduras, and riding a favourite charger, Morzillo – the Black One. It was a

difficult expedition. His force had to thrust through hostile country-side plagued by poisonous insects, through desert, swamp and steaming forest, across arid mountains and fast-running rivers. Fodder for the horses was very scanty and they were reduced to poor condition, Morzillo among them.

The final piece of bad luck for the black charger came when he ran a splinter of wood in his forefoot and was badly lamed. To ride him further would have been the height of cruelty, but the expedition could not be delayed. Cortés therefore placed the Black One in the charge of an Indian chief, making it very clear that he was a most precious animal and that he must be thoroughly cared for till someone was able to return for him.

The cavalcade moved on, and the Indians were left with the prized possession of the god-like general. Anxiously they made the best arrangements they could. Morzillo was given his own attendants, housed in a temple and fed on specially prepared food. But the black horse wanted, not luxury, but simple veterinary knowledge and skill in a country that had none. The conquistador's horse grew gradually weaker and died, amid the lamentations of the frightened chief and his people.

They had failed the Spanish god, the descendant of the sun, and when he returned to claim his own they would not be able to produce him. Only one thing could be done. They could make a model of the horse and pay it the honour that was due. So, in place of the living animal, they carved a curious likeness in stone and, in time, came to rank it with the high gods of the Maya.

Neither Hernan Cortés nor any of his men came back to recover the foundered horse. In time fear was forgotten, but not the fame and power of Morzillo, set, majestically if incongruously, with the rain-god Chac, with the pendulous nose, and the fearsome feathered serpent Kukulcan.

4

Marengo

born *c.* A.D. 1798

Napoleon Bonaparte is stated to have had nearly twenty horses killed under him in battle. His horses were specially trained at a stud-farm at St Cloud, six miles from the centre of Paris. Pictures of the Emperor have made us familiar with his horses, white, cream or grey, and typically Arabian or Barb in breed. Barbs originally came from Barbary – the region of North Africa from Egypt to the Atlantic and from the Sahara Desert to the Mediterranean Sea.

They were a sturdier, rounder type than the Arabian, seldom more than fourteen and a half hands in height. But the terms seem to have been often confused, and it is difficult to decide with some famous early horses whether they were Arabian or Barb. Some writers, for example, maintain that the famous Godolphin Arabian, described in the chapter called 'The Mighty Three', was really a Barb.

In June 1800 Napoleon was campaigning in Italy and encountered a strong Austrian army, under Baron Mélas, in the north at a village called Marengo. Napoleon had left Paris on 6 May and brought his regiments across the Alps. His general Marescot, who had made a reconnaissance of the mountain approaches, told the emperor that the crossing by the St Bernard Pass would be very difficult. 'Difficult? But is it possible?' asked Napoleon. On being told it would be just possible but in the most arduous conditions, Bonaparte answered 'Good. Let us go.'

On the following days [says the French historian Duruy] divisions, gun-carriages, munitions, crossed the pass. The guns, especially those of large calibre and the howitzers, offered great difficulties. They were laid in the hollowed trunks of fir-trees; a hundred men were required for each of these sledges; in the most difficult places music would cheer them or the call to charge would be given; everything crossed successfully.

So, through snow and ice, threatened by avalanches, his munitions and supplies slung across the backs of mules, Napoleon came over the Alps and cut off the Austrian army from their home country. The encounter on 14 June on the plain of Marengo was desperately hard-fought and costly of life.

There were, in fact, three separate battles that day, and the first two were lost by the French. At that point, Count Mélas left the Austrian army in the hands of his deputy and went off to send the news of his triumph round the capitals of Europe. Probably the third battle would have been lost, too, if a message from Napoleon to one of his commanders had not arrived. Before Napoleon knew the where-abouts of the Austrian army he had sent an officer named Desaix, at the head of a division of 6000 troops, to look for it. As the French army was reeling from its earlier disasters, Desaix received a despatch which said 'In God's name, return!' Desaix turned his division and, some four hours later, after a forced march, brought his men to the aid of Napoleon.

Then Napoleon began the third battle. 'My friends,' he said to his soldiers, 'that is enough retreating ...' And he flung Desaix with his 6000 fresh troops on the front of the Austrian column, whilst the rest of the enemy attacked the flanks. Desaix, whose loss can never be sufficiently deplored, fell at the very outset ... But his soldiers threw themselves with the more fury on the Austrians to avenge him. Kellerman charged at the gallop with his squadrons. Marmont suddenly unmasked a battery of large guns. The Austrian column, shaken at its head was broken in two halves. One of them was taken, the other was thrown into disorder. The panic spread to the Austrian cavalry; soon all had fled and Mélas was forced to surrender. Italy was reconquered.

Through all the turmoil of the struggle, Napoleon, short and thick-set, rode on a recently acquired charger, brought into France from Egypt the year before. It stood just over fourteen hands and spoke

Napoleon and Marengo at Wagram during the Austrian campaign, 1809

well for its training, for it remained sure-footed and steady amidst all the thunder of the guns, even when his rider was slightly wounded by a shot which removed part of his left boot.

Napoleon, in fact, was so pleased with the conduct of his white Barb that he named him after the battle, and thenceforward the horse was known as Marengo.

The Emperor had many horses at his command, but none is so closely associated with him as Marengo, none so vividly impressed on the minds of men who saw him and who have since studied his career. Marengo was with him at Austerlitz in December 1805 – the French victory which led William Pitt to say of the map of Europe: 'Roll up that map; it will not be wanted these ten years'; at Jena, five years later, when Napoleon shattered the Prussians. Marengo was with him in defeat, too; in the long disastrous retreat from Moscow in 1812, with the temperature at eighteen degrees of frost, food and vegetation gone, horses and men dying in thousands, and hordes of flying Cossack cavalry swooping on the stragglers; and, finally, at Waterloo, when, then twenty-two years old, he made his last appearance with his Emperor and, it is said, received his eighth wound.

Napoleon used three horses at Waterloo. In his flight to Paris after his defeat by Wellington, he left Marengo behind in a stable at a farmhouse near the battle-field. The horse was captured and brought to England where he was carefully looked after, much fussed over and admired by the curious, and kept at stud near Ely. He outlived his old master by ten years and died in 1831. Five years after, Wellington's charger Copenhagen also died.

5
Copenhagen

born A.D. 1808

God's humble instrument, though meaner clay,
Should share the glory of that glorious day.

As an epitaph*, it is no better and no worse than most. As an epitaph
on a horse it has unusual quality; though the words of his owner,
who was not a poetic man, went nearer to the heart of things: 'There
may be faster horses, no doubt many handsomer, but for bottom and
endurance I never saw his fellow.' 'Bottom' was an expressive word –
to be found in Doctor Johnson's Dictionary – used by our ancestors to
describe stamina and staying power.

The horse's owner might also be considered as a man of consider-
able bottom. He lasted for eighty-three years, in the course of which
he soldiered in the Netherlands, France, Ireland, India, Denmark,
Portugal and Spain; was ambassador in Paris, envoy to Russia, Lord
High Constable of England, Constable of the Tower of London,
Chancellor of Oxford University, Commander-in-Chief and Prime
Minister; and had an important college and the capital of New
Zealand named after him.

*An epitaph to another remarkable horse of the Napoleonic War period survives
at Mara, near Floriand, Malta:
'Here lies the celebrated charger of the late Lieutenant-General Sir Ralph
Abercromby, who was killed at the memorable battle of Alexandria, 21st March
1801, when the noble animal received, on that glorious day, seven musket balls and
two sabre cuts, when he afterwards became the property of John Watson, of Malta,
who placed this stone over his remains, in token of his rare services, peculiar qualities, high spirit, and good temper. This esteemed horse departed this life of miseries,
September 12th 1823, aged 36 years.'

Copenhagen, painted by B. R. Haydon

His powers of blunt speech were such that nearly two columns of the *Oxford Dictionary of Quotations* are given over to him. He was a 'thin, well-made man, apparently of middle stature' and an artist who was commissioned to paint him in later life said 'he looked like an eagle of the gods who had put on human shape, and had got silvery with age and service.' Among his titles, he was Marquess Douro, Earl of Mornington, Condo do Vimeiro, Marquez de Torres Vedras, Duque da Victoria, Duque de Ciudad Rodrigo and Prince of Waterloo.

History knows him best as the Duke of Wellington and has paid him the compliment of a nickname—'the Iron Duke'.

It is safe to say that he is one of the most famous men in English history. It is as true that, in his day, his favourite horse was almost as well known as his great master, familiar to all the troops whom

Wellington led, put on canvas by artists, modelled by sculptors, recorded in diaries and memoirs.

His dam had been schooled in battle, for she had carried a distinguished soldier, Thomas Grosvenor (later general and field-marshal), when he commanded the English brigades at the capture of Copenhagen in 1807, after a two-day bombardment which resulted in the fall of the citadel and the capture of the entire Danish fleet. Her foal, born in 1808, was named Copenhagen in honour of this victory.

Copenhagen was originally trained as a race-horse, but seems to have won only a couple of minor races in the thirteen times he ran in public. He was destined for greater things. He was shipped overseas to serve in the Peninsular War, the struggle between Great Britain and Napoleon that racked Portugal and Spain from 1808–14. It was in 1812 that Wellington saw Copenhagen, now a sturdy chestnut charger, being ridden by a brother officer, Colonel Stewart. The commander-in-chief so liked the look of the horse that he bought him, and thereafter Wellington and Copenhagen were inseparable, in war and peace, for more than twenty years. It was a classic case of the horse and rider partnership Rudyard Kipling described in 'Together':

> ... the one will do what the other demands, although he is beaten and blown,
> And when it is done, they can live through a run that neither could face alone.

The veterans who had served before with the general would see them approaching – the spare upright figure in his plain grey coat buttoned close to the chin, grey pantaloons with boots buckled at the side, and unpretentious steel-mounted sabre, mounted on the spirited chestnut that seemed as much a part of the man as his sword and cocked hat – and a great cheer would go up.

It was not that the horse was an especially magnificent specimen or that the Duke, who was never one for great show, was an impressive rider. It was the dedicated working partnership, the sure impression of hard toil and danger shared, rather than any dash or bravura, that made their mark.

35

A contemporary wrote:

The Duke of Wellington never shared the taste of his companions-in-arms for parade chargers and high-school horsemanship. The through-bred* chestnut Copenhagen, which carried him so stoutly ... was only fifteen hands high. His horse was a hunter class of animal, a good walker, ridden in a snaffle bridle, like a huntsman's horse, without a thought of showing off the animal's paces.

In that lifetime of action, the event above all others associated with Wellington is the battle of Waterloo, fought on 18 June 1815 and generally reckoned one of the decisive battles in the history of the world. It was Napoleon's last desperate throw. Early in March he had escaped from the island of Elba where he had been sent by the Allies after his abdication in April 1814. France had suffered greatly at the hands of her soldier-emperor. He had won great victories, but at a terrible price in terms of French blood and treasure. But as he moved through the countryside back to Paris, though many men of good sense knew in their hearts that the adventure was doomed to failure, the magic of Napoleon's name and presence won them again. Defeat and disaster were forgotten and his old officers and regiments rallied to join him in his last march to meet Wellington. Born in the same year, commissioned as officers in the same year, the two generals had never met before through all their long campaigns.

The battle began at about 11.30 in the morning.

It was one of the bitterest, most heroic struggles in history – one that saved Europe, but at a terrible price. No official returns have been made of the French losses; but at the end of the day nearly 15,000 of Wellington's army were killed or wounded, as well as 7000 Prussians.

Through the day-long din and smoke of that day, the Duke on Copenhagen moved amongst his men, upright, imperturbable, en-couraging. The murmur 'Stand to your front – here's the Duke!'

*To be quite accurate, Copenhagen was not quite a thoroughbred, since his grand-dam was a half-bred hunter.

would stiffen the most confused and battered column and bring it back to parade-like discipline. To one hard-pressed battalion which the French guns were pounding incessantly he said:

'Hard pounding this, gentlemen: we will try who can pound the longest.'

On the day before the battle, Wellington had ridden Copenhagen for some ten hours. He himself wrote:

On June 17th, before 10 o'clock I got on Copenhagen's back – so much to do that neither he nor I were still for many minutes together. I never drew bit and he never had a morsel in his mouth till 8 p.m. The poor beast I myself saw stabled and fed in the village of Waterloo.

On the day of battle he rode him again from early dawn till night – an even longer period, of some seventeen hours. At the end of it all when, grey with fatigue and saddened with slaughter, the Duke came back to the village of Waterloo, picking his way through the moonlit lanes and fields filled with dead and dying men, there were still those who lifted their heads to cheer the silent man on the chestnut horse.

After nearly thirty hours riding in two days, with little pause for food and water, Copenhagen still had sufficient spirit to lash out when Wellington swung himself wearily from the saddle. The flying hooves narrowly missed the general and nearly accomplished what the French guns had failed to do. The next day Copenhagen broke loose and rampaged through the streets of Brussels before the sweating soldiers caught up with him and brought him back, snorting and defiant.

Copenhagen was eventually retired to the Duke's estate at Stratfield Saye. The Duke always had an eye for a pretty face, and the greatest compliment he could pay was to let an attractive visitor ride Copenhagen. Lady Frances Shelley wrote:

I dined at three o'clock in order to ride with the Duke, who offered to mount me on Copenhagen. A charming ride of two hours. But I found Copenhagen the most difficult horse to sit of any I have ridden. If the Duke had not been there, I should have been frightened. He said: 'I believe you think the glory greater than the pleasure in riding him!'

In his later years, the Duke would often appear suddenly tired and old. The painter Haydon described him at the age of seventy, when he first appeared in the morning as 'looking extremely worn; his skin drawn tight over his face; his eye was watery and aged; his head nodded a little. He looked like an aged eagle beginning to totter from his perch.'

As a matter of fact, Wellington outlived the painter by six years. And whatever his weariness, one thing could always bring the flash back to his eye, the flush to his cheek, the firm line to his jaw – to talk of Copenhagen, who had shared his greatest triumphs.

The Horse on Show

It was a general opinion, and even some of good wisdom have maintained the assertion, that it was not possible to bee done by a Horse that which Cutall did, but by the assistance of the Devil.
– Gervase Markham

Introduction

Ignoring the arguments for and against the training of performing animals, a question on which strong feelings are often aroused, it seems fairly certain that only a minority of horses (and those not always the best bred) are adaptable to such training.

Two other things are reasonably clear: first, that the best results have been achieved by infinite patience and kindness rather than by cruelty; and second, that some men have a special gift for establishing a *rapport* or sympathetic relationship with horses, even to the extent of holding jealously guarded secrets. The greatest jockeys probably have this special understanding. Certainly Philip Astley, in one of the chapters in this section, had it. We know nothing of the training methods used by Banks, the other showman described here.

One of the most curious methods of horse control, apparently practised through the centuries, is that known as 'jading'. Horses are very sensitive to smells and become very awkward if they are confronted with one that they find objectionable. There are many cases on record, right up to recent times, of horsemen and countryfolk 'jading' a horse; that is, bringing it to a standstill by treating the ground in front of it, or smearing some part of the horse itself (chest, nostrils, forelegs) with the objectionable substance. It might be done to win a wager, impress the simple-minded, or even as an act of revenge for some hurt or misdeed. Whatever the motive, the horse would stand stock still, stubbornly refusing to move an inch lest it moved into the imagined zone of the offensive smell.

Clovis, who lived from about the year 466 till 511 and was king of the eight separate dominions into which old Gaul was divided, was nearly defeated in 496 by a tribe called the Alemanni, on the plains of the Tolbiac, twenty-four miles from Cologne. Edward Gibbon, the historian of the last days of the Roman Empire, records:

After the Gothic victory, Clovis made rich offerings to St Martin of Tours. He wished to redeem his warhorse by the gift of one hundred pieces of gold, but the enchanted steed could not move from the stable till the price of his redemption had been doubled. This miracle provoked the king to exclaim: *Vere, B. Martimus est bonus in auxilio, sed carus in negotio.* (Truly, St Martin is a good friend in need, but he's an expensive one to bargain with.)

George Ewart Evans, in a fine book called *The Pattern Under the Plough*, suggests that, in fact, the horse had been 'jaded' by the astute priests, who used their skill to such an extent that they were able to extract the double ransom money from Clovis. Evans gives another classic example of the jading of a horse. A very knowledgeable and experienced Suffolk horseman was riding home when he came across a younger man, who had made himself unpopular by continual boasting, in great trouble. One horse in his team insisted on backing, and the other was resolutely pulling forward. The older man, William Rookyard, told the story afterwards:

'"Wait here a minute, bo" I said; "I'll tell you what: you've been a braggin' again, haven't you?"

"No," said the first, "I haven't said a lot."

"I told you," said Rookyard, "you must not brag what you can do, because there's allus somebody as good a man as yourself."

He climbed down from his own wagon and went across to the struggling horse. He went on:

"So I just went afront there with my milk and vinegar; rubbed it in my palm and fingers; and then I rubbed it inside the horses' nose and round their nostrils. I then said to this young horseman: "Now hop on your wagon and be off!" and he done so."'

Rookyard had apparently used a 'drawing' or 'calling' oil to counteract the jading preparation. These oils would neutralize the objectionable compound if rubbed over it, and would attract the horse rather than repel it. If the ground only had been treated with the jading preparation, it was enough to back the horse clear of the infected area.

The young boaster had been taught an effective lesson; though it is doubtful if, at the same time, he learnt the secret, for the old horsemen guarded the mystery of their preparations. Some of the ingredients sound so grim that it is understandable that any self-respecting horse should steadfastly refuse to have anything to do with them.

6
The Horse with the Silver Shoes

c. A.D. 1590

For a horse to be written about by journalists and sporting writers is common enough; for it to be celebrated by poets and dramatists is more rare; and when it is mentioned by nearly every great writer of the day, it must be a very unusual sort of horse altogether.

Such a horse was Morocco, sometimes spelt Marocco or Maroccus. He lived in the reigns of Elizabeth I and James I, a period in our history which produced a group of writers whose greatness has never been equalled since; and most of them thought it worth while to take note of Morocco.

Shakespeare refers to 'the dancing horse' in *Love's Labour's Lost*. The poet–priest John Donne made reference to him in 1593. Ben Jonson knew all about Morocco. So did Jonson's rival Thomas Dekker and 'that proud Lucifer' Sir Walter Raleigh, whose *History of the World* was published in 1614. In 1595 a special little pamphlet was written called *A Ballad Showing the Strange Qualities of a Young Nagg call Morocco*.

Morocco was born about 1590, probably at Newmarket, the market town in Suffolk which has been known as a horse-racing centre since the time of James I and which was a focus for breeders and dealers before that.

His owner was a Scotsman named Thomas Banks, or Bankes, who had a varied career. At one time he was in the service of Robert Devereux, Earl of Essex, the favourite of Queen Elizabeth who finally wearied the Queen with his arrogance and paid for it with his life in 1601. Banks must have lived to a great age, for he seems to have been in business as a wine-merchant in Cheapside as late as 1665,

when the Great Plague swept through London. Two things about him are quite certain – he must have had a way with animals and he was himself a superb horseman, for only thus could he have trained and ridden Morocco in the manner that made such an impression on all who saw them. Indeed, it may be said that he was too skilful, for he earned himself and his horse a deal of trouble.

We know few details about Morocco, other than that he was a bay of middle height and was a curtal. Curtal is an old word meaning having a short or docked tail. A curtal dog was one owned by a person not allowed to hunt in the lord's coverts and forests. It arose from the theory that a dog cannot run or hunt properly unless its tail is full length. A curtal friar was probably so-called because he wore a short frock.

Whether or not a cropped tail made a hunting dog less efficient, it certainly made no difference to the horse Morocco. Trick horses are fairly common in history; but Banks's Horse, as he was usually known, was something quite outstanding.

Morocco could dance a jig, walk on his hind legs, not only forwards, but backwards and in circles. He could rear up at command, kneel and lie down. But he could go much further than this with the aid of his expert owner. In these days we can still marvel, but we understand a little more about skilful signalling between master and beast and give credit to superb showmanship. We don't necessarily want to know the answer, but we don't believe in magic as those who watched Banks and Morocco often did. Banks would have a dice thrown, and Morocco would immediately rap out with his elegant hoof the number of spots that came uppermost. Similarly, he would tap out the number of pence in a shilling. Shown a glove, he would daintily sniff it and then, led round by Banks, would pick out the owner from among the spectators.

Having made a great reputation in England, the showman took his famous horse overseas and created such an impression that he and his horse were suspected of being in league with the devil. Banks was thrown into prison on at least one occasion and on another escaped only by a particularly amazing trick. To convince his accusers that there was nothing evil about him or his horse, he induced Morocco to kneel before a man wearing a crucifix in his hat and then to rise and kiss the cross. No greater proof of piety could be imagined.

Did Banks plant an assistant among the onlookers, or was it just luck that he spotted someone with the crucifix in his hat?

Whichever it was, Banks was less fortunate in Italy, the next country in which he performed. The details are uncertain, but it seems likely that Morocco did not come home again to England. One record states that the Pope ordered both man and horse to be destroyed as allies of the devil. If this is so, Banks himself was either pardoned or managed to escape. But Morocco passed from the records of history and lived on only in the pages of the great writers he had so impressed.

It is said that he was shod with silver shoes. Such a gesture would have been quite in line with Banks's masterly showmanship. Gervase Markham (1568?–1637), one of the first English writers on the horse, boasted that he could have taught a horse to perform any of Morocco's tricks in less than a month. But Ben Jonson called Gervase Markham 'a base fellow', and he was probably right.

7
Astley's and 'The Little Learned Military Horse'

c. A.D. 1770–1814

The London directories round about the year 1800 have a short entry: 'Astley's Theatre, Westminster Bridge Road.' The theatre has now disappeared and its site is occupied by a modern block of flats in Lambeth.

Philip Astley, born in 1742, had a varied career. He was apprenticed to a cabinet-maker, but soon tired of this unadventurous life and enlisted in the Light Dragoons. Here he became an experienced breaker-in of horses and rose to the rank of sergeant-major.

When, at the age of twenty-six, he was demobilized, he determined to put his knowledge of horses to good account and to offer his services as riding-master to the nobility and gentry. For this purpose he needed funds to build a riding school, so he put on an exhibition of horses and horsemanship at Lambeth. The riding-school venture failed, so Astley decided on another. If he could not run an exclusive training school for the upper classes, why not found a place of amusement for the general population?

So, in 1770, he opened an equestrian circus at Westminster, later to become known as Astley's Theatre. Over the years, with varying success, he established nineteen such theatres, including establishments in Dublin and Paris. His horses became much in demand for performances at Covent Garden Theatre and, indeed, had plays especially written for them. A critic wrote of one: '"Timour the Tartar," written expressly for the equestrian troop, is, as a literary production, contemptible; it is only a spectacle;' but, 'The feats of these animals drew crowded houses, and the exhibition was the subject of surprise, as well as the object of delight'.

Astley's Amphitheatre, as seen by Pugin and Rowlandson in 1808

Philip Astley was not only a clever showman. He was a great trainer of horses and, unusually for his day, a gentle and understanding one. Richard Lawrence, a well-known veterinary surgeon and writer on horses, who had strong views on humanitarian treatment, was able to write of Astley:

When the rider quarrels with his horse, he is generally the dupe of his passions, and the fray commonly ends to his disadvantage. Whenever you see a man beating any animal, it is at least ten to one that the man is in the wrong, and the animal in the right. A good-natured clever man may teach a horse anything, and it is a very mistaken notion that those horses which perform so many dexterous tricks at Astley's, and places of that description, are brought to execute them by violent means. The fact is, they are taught by gentle means only, and by rewarding them at the moment they obey; hence they become accustomed by habit to combine the recollection of the

48

reward with the performance of the trick, and it becomes a pleasure to them instead of labour.

Describing Astley's horses, Lawrence went on:

They would perform the figure of a minuet; lie down at the word of command; and, during a sham battle, fall as if dead, and not stir till they had permission. Gentle means, as already observed, were chiefly adopted for their instruction; but . . . they had an imperious master, who would suffer none of his servants to be idle, as the following anecdote, (never before published, and which was witnessed by the writer) will sufficiently testify:

Perceiving a man in his band suddenly cease performing on his violin, Mr Astley exclaimed, 'Sir, Sir! why are not you playing?' 'It is a *rest*, replied the man, meaning a *rest in music*. 'A *rest*!' exclaimed Mr A. 'but, Sir, I pay you a weekly salary, and by — I'll suffer no man to *rest* that's in my employment!' There is no doubt but he was exceedingly kind to his horses, but he certainly would not let them rest till they performed their daily tasks.

One of the familiar exhibits at Astley's own theatre was the Gibraltar Charger, the horse given to the sergeant-major by General Eliott when he was discharged from the 15th Light Dragoons. The old war-horse 'posed serene amid a display of fireworks', just as he had behaved in his days of battle. Another of Astley's most famous horses was Billy, known as 'The Little Learned Military Horse'.

Billy's career lasted for nearly forty years and he had the distinction of serving as a model for the famous animal painter Abraham Cooper.

Billy was trained to count by listening to the little click of his trainer's finger-nails and tapping a corresponding number with his hoof. The same method was probably used with Banks's Horse, whose story is told in the previous chapter. On one occasion, Astley nearly lost Billy. He lent him to another showman who was badly in debt and who had the horse taken away in payment. Billy was bought by a tradesman and put between the shafts of a cart. Fortunately Astley saw him and recognized him. He clicked his nails and, doubtless in pleasure at meeting his old master, Billy responded so vigorously that he nearly upset the cart in his excitement.

Billy 'would mark the name of Astley, letter by letter, in the earth; tell gold from silver and ladies from gentlemen; take a handkerchief from its owner and "die" rather than fight for the Spaniard.'

Even in old age, he still took pleasure in displaying some of his old tricks. He would dutifully wash his feet in a pond of water, could take off his own saddle, and even remove a boiling kettle from a fire.

The Horse in Sport

Philip of Macedon reckoned a horse-race
won at Olympus among his three fearful
felicities.
– Sir Philip Sidney

Introduction

Horse-racing is one of the oldest sports enjoyed by mankind and there is no doubt that races have taken place ever since the first wild horses were tamed by our far-away ancestors. In literature, racing is mentioned in the Iliad, the Greek poem written more than 2500 years ago. Early races were probably impromptu and haphazard affairs; but, as time went on, matches between riders grew into organized meetings regulated by strict rules.

In this country, though races had undoubtedly taken place through long centuries before, the reign of Henry VIII is generally taken as the period when properly organized race meetings occur on any scale. Queen Elizabeth kept a breeding stud and is recorded as attending races at Croydon, Surrey, in 1585, 1587 and 1588.

Chester is one of the few places for which early written records exist of race meetings. In the British Museum is a document giving details of one such event in 1610. We do not know the names of the horses; but, preparatory to the race, a colourful procession, in which horses and riders were named after various legendary characters, vices and virtues, wound its way through the streets between the half-timbered houses, watched over by the castle and the red sandstone cathedral. At one point, though the record does not explain how the feat was accomplished, the organizers caused 'one called Mercury to descend from above in a cloud, his wings and all other matters in pomp, and heavenly music with him.'

There used to be a common expression 'to bear the bell', meaning to be first or to carry off the prize. This had its origin in the early custom of awarding small gold or silver bells to the winners of horse-races. At Chester, it was Robert Amory, ironmonger and sheriff, who caused 'three silver bells to be made of good value, which bells be appointed to be run for with horses.' The race was to be run on St George's Day from the Roodee (the wide green space by the River Dee, beneath the south-west wall of the city) to the Watergate, the first arrival to have 'the beste bell', the next 'the seconde bell' and so on, the winners to keep the bells for a year, then return them to be run for again.

Robert Amory put on a brave show for the citizens, at what must have been considerable cost, and his wish that the races 'be continued for ever' has so far been respected. The annual race meeting is still held in May, but much of the glory has departed. There are no silver bells to greet the victors and, alas, no Mercury descending from above in a cloud.

Ben Jonson wrote: 'They say Princes learn no art truly but the art of horsemanship. The reason is, the brave beast is no flatterer. He will throw a Prince as soon as his groom.' It has certainly been true that good horsemanship has always been reckoned a necessary accomplishment of English kings and queens, as the royal family still demonstrates today in the persons of Elizabeth II and Princess Anne.

Not many monarchs, however, have ridden in horse-races where wagers were laid. One who did was Charles II, who was among the best horsemen in England. His teacher said that he never forced or ill-treated his mount, though the king was willing to wager he would ride bare-backed any horse brought to him. Charles raced on a number of occasions at Newmarket. On 12 October 1671, riding Woodcock, he rode against one of the Gentlemen of the Bedchamber, Mr Elliott, who, though he was mounted on a horse called Flatfoot, was nimble enough to beat the king. Two days later his majesty had better luck. Riding for a flagon as prize, he beat a field which included the same Mr Elliott and the Duke of Monmouth. The King rode another winner at Newmarket in 1684, the year before he died.

This royal patronage over the centuries is one of the chief reasons

A race over the long course at Newmarket, from an engraving by Peter Tillemans dedicated to George II when he was Prince of Wales

why horse-racing has always been a popular spectacle in England and has long been known as 'the sport of kings'.

8
Lorenzo the Magnificent's Firefly
A.D. 1485

A place famous for horse-races in the Middle Ages was Siena, the Italian walled city in central Tuscany. Siena preserves much of its medieval atmosphere, and travellers can still watch the famous 'Palio', the horse-race held twice a year, at the beginning of July and in the middle of August, in the old square known as the Piazza del Campo.

On these occasions a brilliant procession of people in medieval costume precedes a wild and dangerous race by bare-back riders representing the ten divisions of the city, and the prize is a silken banner called the 'pallium'.

The original meaning of palio was a mantle or woollen cloak, and the winner of a horse-race was often given a new cloak. Then the race itself, in Italy, became known by this name. An account survives of a palio in Siena as early as 1485 in the diary of a man-about-town named Luca Landucci, whose brother Gostanzo owned a Barbary horse called Draghetto.

Draghetto had built up an impressive record, winning twenty races in four years, from October 1481 to June 1485. Then he was brought to Siena to take part in the palio and to face severe competition, not only because there was a strong field but because one of his opponents was a horse named *La Lucciola* (the Firefly), owned by no less a person than Lorenzo de' Medici. As it turned out, this proved an unlooked-for complication.

The Medici were one of the most famous families in history, rising from being merchants and bankers to Dukes and Princes in Florence and Tuscany and, through their financial interests, playing an important role in the whole of Europe. Their coat-of-arms, displaying golden plates or 'bezants', still survives in the three golden balls often seen hanging as a sign outside pawnbrokers' shops, a reminder of the power of the Medici as bankers and lenders of money.

Among them all, there was none more famous than Lorenzo de' Medici (1449–92), known as 'the Magnificent' from his wealth and the splendour of his court. He was a complex character, like so many Renaissance princes, immoral and ruthless, ruling with the aid of an army of spies and assassins, yet given to writing sensitive poetry; knowing a great deal about painting, sculpture and architecture; attracting to his court the greatest scholars of Italy; lavishing money on festivals and public displays, but himself eating and dressing simply and refusing his daughters permission to wear fine fabrics; passionately fond of violets 'so fresh and fair of hue ... plucked by the hand of innocence', yet capable of throwing those same innocents into prison.

One writer described him as 'tall and of a noble presence', with 'an ugly face, short sight, dark skin and hair, sallow cheeks and an extraordinary large mouth.' His wife, Donna Clarice Orsini, said he was 'short-sighted, flat-nosed and deprived of all sense of smell.' For this defect Lorenzo declared he was grateful, because more smells were offensive than delightful. It was probably true in the Middle Ages.

Whatever his looks, there is no doubt of the respect and fear Lorenzo commanded, and the 1485 horse-race at Siena provided a small example.

Luca Landucci wrote in his diary:

When he [his brother Gostanzo] went to race at Siena, there was a tie between his horse and one belonging to Lorenzo de' Medici, called *La Lucciola*, that of Gostanzo being in reality one head's length in advance of the other. And the people who were present declared he had won, and told him to go to the magistrate, and they would bear witness. Gostanzo, however, refused to do this out of respect for Lorenzo and, as it happened, Lorenzo was declared the winner.

Siena was, in fact, an unlucky course for Gostanzo. On another occasion, riding Draghetto, he was a bowshot in front of all his rivals and dismounted at the finishing line. But, while he proudly waited for the prize, another horse rushed past whose rider, supported by a number of onlookers, swore that Draghetto had not actually passed the post. Gostanzo therefore lost the palio, which, as his brother very mildly records, 'was most unfortunate, as my brother had such a good horse'.

9
The Mighty Three
c. A.D. 1689–1728

The term 'thoroughbred' would probably be interpreted by most people now as meaning 'pedigree' or truly or purely bred. They would be right, but its more exact meaning is 'through bred', that is, bred right through a long line of pure stock back to a known ancestor.

In the case of race-horses, it is an extraordinary fact that thorough-breds all over the world, not only in Europe, but in North and South America, in Australia and throughout the dominions of Great Britain, all trace back in direct line to three English race-horses or, more accurately, to three horses from the Middle East introduced into England in the space of about forty years.

Eastern, and especially Arabian, horses have been famous from the beginning of recorded history. King Solomon (*c.* 986–932 B.C.) is reported to have had a thousand wives. He was also a keen man on horses; for the Book of Kings tells us:

> And Solomon gathered together chariots and horsemen: and he had a thousand and four hundred chariots, and twelve thousand horsemen . . . and Solomon had horses brought out of Egypt . . . and a chariot came up and went out of Egypt for six hundred shekels of silver, and an horse for an hundred and fifty.

A nineteenth-century writer gives seven different colours for Arabian horses: clear bay (*ahmar*); brown bay (*edhem*); sorrel, or chestnut (*ashekwar*); white (*abiadh*); pure grey (*azrak*); mottled grey (*raktha*); and bluish grey (*akhhar*). Blacks (*aswad*) and light bays (*ashehab*) were apparently unknown in Arabia, though they were to be found in other countries such as Persia and Mongolia.

The same writer says of the early races of horses that:

The races of Nejed are commonly regarded as the noblest; those of the Hejjaz as the handsomest; those of the Yemen as the most durable; those of Syria as the richest in colour; those of Mesopotamia as the most quiet; those of Egypt as the swiftest; those of Barbary as the most prolific, and those of Persia and Kurdestan as the most warlike.

The first of the famous trio that laid the foundations of all modern bloodstock was the so-called Byerley Turk, named after Captain Robert Byerley, an adventurous young soldier who took himself off to fight in Turkey where, it is believed, he captured his famous horse from the enemy. It has therefore come down in history as the Byerley Turk, though the stallion was almost certainly Arabian in

The Byerley Turk, painted by John Wootton. Courtesy of Fores Ltd

origin. After returning to England, Captain Byerley was sent to Ireland in 1689 to fight in King William's war there. It is related that his regiment, the Queen Dowager's Cuirassiers, wore sea-green uniforms and that they reinforced the colour scheme by wearing bunches of green leaves in their hats and plaiting their horses' manes and tails with green ribbons.

Byerley, by this time promoted Colonel, set off on a lone reconnoitring expedition and, scouting far ahead of the main force, suddenly found himself surrounded by a troop of horsemen wearing, not the green of the Cuirassiers, but the white flashes of the Irish enemy. Byerley turned the Turk, touched him with his spurs and disappeared at such speed that he left his pursuers far behind and rejoined his regiment in safety.

The second great sire was the so-called Darley Arabian, which was bought as a yearling in Aleppo, Syria, and imported into England in

The Darley Arabian, from a painting by J. N. Sartorius

about 1706. The Arabs had a confusing custom of naming horses after their owners, which naturally changed from time to time, so that the name altered too. The same system was introduced into England for a time, making it extremely difficult, sometimes, to trace a horse's origins. Fortunately the Darley Arabian never changed hands after his arrival. Darley's horse was a bay with a white blaze. It is a strange fact that Darley, when he bought the horse, was not at all certain that it was of a type that would be welcomed at home. He would have been amazed had he been able to see the modern Stud Book which records the ancestry of all thoroughbred horses. In the 1940s there were 7000 brood mares in the Stud Book that carried the blood of the Darley Arabian.

The third member was the Godolphin Arabian, imported about 1728.

There are conflicting stories of his origins, one, of very doubtful accuracy, saying that he was found drawing a water-cart in Paris. What is certain, however, is that he was presented to Lord Godolphin, an officer of George I's household, and remained in his possession for the rest of his days.

The Godolphin Arabian was a brown bay, $14\frac{1}{2}$ or 15 hands high, with some white on his off heel. The only picture of him drawn from life was by John Wootton (1668?–1765), a famous painter of race-horses. It was discovered by Lady Wentworth, who says the portrait shows a pure Arabian type, with 'tapering head, small ears, a large full eye, level quarters and high set tail'. The horse seems to have formed a close friendship with a cat, for one appears with him in many early pictures.

Two things must be added about these great horses.

It is sometimes assumed that, because these are the three to which all modern thoroughbreds are traced, they were the first to be brought into England. In fact, no one can say with certainty when the Arabian first arrived. It is known that James I bought one for 500 guineas, but even this was probably a comparatively late arrival. It is more logical to suppose that the Crusaders, who had seen some-

63

The Godolphin Arabian, from an engraving by George Stubbs, published in 1794

thing of the quality of the Eastern horses in Egypt and the Holy Land, brought some home. Others recorded in England before the Byerley Turk are the Helmsley Turk, belonging to the Duke of Buckingham, and the White Turk, which was owned by Oliver Cromwell's stud-master. In all, according to the first Stud Book, published in 1781, 174 Eastern sires had been imported in the previous 200 years; but of these only the three described above have kept their lines of descent pure and intact to this day.

The second fact is that, although so much merit is attached to Eastern ancestry, the English race-horse, for a very long time, has been able to beat an Arab easily, except perhaps over long distances where extra stamina is required. The Byerley Turk, the Darley Arabian and the Godolphin Arabian passed on great qualities; but they would not stand the slightest chance if matched with only a moderate English thoroughbred today. The English climate, careful feeding and centuries of controlled breeding have seen to that.

10
Lottery

c. A.D. 1830–1850

The early 1830s saw a variety of interesting events in England. William IV – 'a little, old, red-nosed, weather-beaten, jolly-looking person' – had come to the throne late in life; the Liverpool and Manchester Railway had opened; the Great Reform Bill was passed, giving a much fairer system of sending members to Parliament; the great Duke of Wellington, hero of Waterloo, so far fell in popularity through his opposition to this reform that the crowds in London hurled bricks through his window and hooted him on the anniversary of the battle.

Up in Yorkshire, a less dramatic event occurred, but one that influenced the lives of a great many people and made history of a sort. A brown half-bred horse was born on a farm near Thirsk. They called him Chance, though he didn't keep the name for long. It was before the days of the careful regulation and recording of horses' names and Chance soon had his changed to Lottery, which seems much the same sort of thing.

After winning a race in 1834, but not showing promise out of the ordinary, the brown horse was sent in 1836 to be sold at the great fair held at Horncastle in Lincolnshire. Horse fairs were the chief means of buying horses of every description, for hunting, driving in harness or working. In 1807 the *Monthly Mirror* recorded 4000 horses were offered for sale each day and that, since the fair continued for ten days, about 16,000 were sold in all. By the middle of the century, Horncastle was being called 'the greatest mart for horses, with the exception of those intended for racing purposes that is to be found in England.'

At Horncastle a ruddy-complexioned farmer named John Elmore, well known as a dealer and sportsman, liked the look of Lottery and bought him for 120 gold sovereigns. He was not a handsome horse, being 'leggy, narrow, short in his quarters, and his general appearance led to the idea that he would very probably go back to the place from whence he came', but Elmore had a good eye and saw something beneath the rough exterior. Elmore had something else – a young rider named Jem Mason who became one of the finest riders in England and who, incidentally, married his employer's daughter. After Lottery had been brought home to Elmore's farm near Harrow in Middlesex, Jem Mason rode the horse a great deal and, with his sensitive hands and understanding of the mettle of his mount, turned him into a fine, beautifully controlled hunter.

Lottery (on right) with Jem Mason up

Elmore began to enter Lottery for steeplechases, first at small local tracks, then at more important ones. After several successes, in 1839 the horse was entered for a newly organized race called the Grand National Steeplechase at Liverpool. It was a tough course, consisting of 29 fences on the two circuits and including several frightening obstacles. The worst was a stone wall nearly five feet high. News of the race had spread throughout Britain and many of the greatest horses in the country were sent up. On the day of the race, Tuesday 26 February, the roads were jammed with a motley procession of horses, vehicles and race-goers on foot. The grandstand was so packed that movement was almost impossible and the refreshment booths soon ran out of food and drink.

But the discomforts were all forgotten in the excitement of the race. It was the half-bred brown horse called Lottery that, jumping smoothly and superbly throughout, came home an easy winner. When they came to the five-foot wall, the leading horse refused it; the next made a poor jump and clouted it with his hind legs. Lottery cleared it with 'a tremendous flying jump, enough to have cleared a fair brook on either side.' According to all accounts, he was still so lively at the end that, over the final hurdle, he accomplished a leap of thirty-three feet.

It was the beginning of a great year for Lottery, in which he won three other important steeplechases. At the end of the season, the Elmores held a reception in his honour. House and gardens at Uxenden near Harrow were gay with lights, graceful dresses and the gleam of jewellery. Tables were laden with food and drink and the toast of the evening was the brown horse Lottery.

He replied to the toast in suitable manner. The chief dining-table had been set in the garden, all the best china and silver gracing the snowy table-linen. Lottery was ridden at the table and cleared it in great style amidst prolonged applause.

His reputation became such that he was barred from even entering certain race-meetings for fear that he would keep away other owners.

But his triumphant career continued. In the next year, every time with Jem Mason up, Lottery won six great races. Thereafter he gradually became less successful, chiefly because of his exclusion from courses, or because officials made him carry crushing weights to give others a chance. These slowed him so much by the end of the gruelling four-mile courses that he was almost forced out of racing. Lottery's last appearance was at Windsor on 8 April 1844 which, as a fitting curtain to a great career, he won.

His later years had none of the glory and applause, but were probably happy enough. He was ridden as a hack by an owner who was very attached to him and he finished up in a cart team. But his reputation lives on as, in the words of a sporting writer of the 1860s, 'the best horse that ever looked through a bridle'.

11

The Grey Horse of Martinvast

c. A.D. 1890

It was a long-established belief that grey among horses was a slow colour. Samuel Sidney quoted 'a very competent authority' of 1855 who had calculated that:

In the previous thirty years the Derby had been won by sixteen bays, seven chestnuts, and seven browns; the St Leger by seventeen bays, eight browns, and five chestnuts. Since that time the proportionate number of bays has been maintained, the number of chestnuts has increased, the number of browns diminished, and *no grey or roan has won either of these great stakes.*

Other serious students maintained that 'speed and bay colour are inseparable'; that supreme speed could be looked for only in a bay with a white star; and that grey, since it could never be the colour of a Derby winner, would disappear from the track.

In 1884 a horse was foaled that was destined to smash this legend for good. The strange thing about him, quite apart from this matter of colour, was that he got off to a disastrous start in life and developed late.

The grey colt, named Le Sancy, was bred by a foreign owner, Baron de Schikler, who wished to develop a great stud of horses on his estates in France and who imported the best English strains he could buy. For about twenty years the Baron had no spectacular success with his Martinvast Stud, despite all his careful breeding. Then, in 1884, Le Sancy was foaled.

The little colt was a spirited animal, as full of curiosity about the world in which he found himself as most youngsters. His curiosity, in fact, nearly finished him for good in his first few months in the pad-

dock. Examining a stile, which probably gave promise of access to a wider world on the other side of the boundary fence, he threw up his head and somehow got caught by the jaw. His violent jerkings and twistings nearly strangled him. Fortunately a passer-by saw his struggles and, after a great effort, managed to free the colt. The stud groom was called and he arrived to find Le Sancy stretched on the ground apparently lifeless. The groom worked on him and managed to bring him round, only to find that the colt's jaws were dislocated. A veterinary surgeon was hastily fetched from Chantilly, but he shook his head and said nothing could be done.

After that, Le Sancy spent a miserable two months. While he was still with his mother things were not too difficult, but after he was weaned it was a pathetic sight to see the leggy grey colt trying to cope with corn with his dislocated jaws.

Then the miracle happened. As he was forlornly doing his best to work some corn round his mouth, the jaws suddenly snapped back into place.

After this Le Sancy made rapid strides, but was some time in reaching his full development. Not until he was six years old did he reach his peak as a race-horse. But it had been worth waiting for. When he was five he was first at the post on ten successive occasions. When he was six he ran in nine races and won every time. Despite all the statistics and the pronouncements of the experts, a grey had arrived who could beat the best, whether they were bays, browns, chestnuts or any other hue.

After that, other greys killed the old belief for good. In 1936, a grey named Mahmoud not only won the Derby but did so in record time –2 minutes 33.8 seconds, or an average speed of over 35 m.p.h. In 1946 another grey, Airborne, won 'in slashing style, coming roaring up from nowhere'.

And no one interested in horses will ever forget Steve Donoghue's famous 'rocking horse', the incredible Tetrarch, that he declared was the world's fastest horse. Of his first racing gallop when in training his trainer wrote:

I had three in that gallop: a couple of two year olds that I knew went a bit, and an old horse that was giving away 21 lb. As this was the first time the Tetrarch had been really jumped off, I told the boy who was riding him to lie beside the others and, when he commenced to tire, to ease him up. Imagine my surprise to see, after three furlongs, the old horse and the speedy two year olds hard ridden, but the Tetrarch two lengths ahead of the rest and still going at apparently half-speed. The boy on his back was doing nothing to urge his mount forward, though the others were all out.

In the opinion of some the Tetrarch was 'the most remarkable horse ever foaled'. He always ran straight out in front of the field, a habit which, Steve Donoghue thought, would have stopped him ever winning the Derby. Unfortunately it was never put to the test. In 1913 the grey rocking horse ran and won seven times. He was never beaten. But the next year the First World War broke out and the Tetrarch never raced again.

The Tetrarch, painted by H. F. Lucas Lucas in 1914

12
Arkle

born A.D. 1957

Arkle was not a particularly impressive horse when he was foaled, and he nearly abruptly ended his career by almost severing his leg on some barbed wire, an accident from which he always carried the scar. One of his early stable jockeys said of him: 'He looked the worst of all the four year olds who arrived that season. He was unfurnished. And he moved bad.' Another said of his ungainly hind leg movement: 'He moved so terribly behind that you could drive a wheelbarrow through his hind legs.'

It was a strange beginning to the career of the most famous horse of his day. But two things he could obviously do well – he could stay a difficult course and he could jump.

After several try-outs he was entered as a five year old for a three-mile novice steeplechase at Navan and found himself up against twenty-six other runners. He stayed comfortably behind most of the field nearly all the way. Then suddenly, the lean, awkward fellow opened up. The race looked already won; but the leading jockey, already hearing the cheers for the winner, to his amazement suddenly saw a horse streaking by him at an incredible pace as though he had just started instead of finishing a hard three miles. The crowd were so surprised at Arkle's win that the result was greeted almost with silence.

He did little more that season, and he was soon to take a bad fall. This showed his third great gift. He always learned from his mistakes and never had to be shown twice. In fact, he never fell again.

After his win at Navan he lost two races; then began his incredible blaze of glory. In the next season he was entered for seven races – and

Arkle, from a painting by Cashman

Arkle wins the S.G.B. Handicap Chase by fifteen lengths during his last great month, December 1966

won seven, including two Gold Cups at Fairyhouse and Punchestown. Of his next ten races, he won nine including, in England, the Hennessy Gold Cup at Newbury and the Gold Cup at Cheltenham. Out of seventeen consecutive races he had thundered home first sixteen times, the remaining occasion being one on which he was not fully fit.

The lean, awkward horse had become a national hero. In the process he had filled out and taken on a more handsome appearance. And he seemed to know it. There were times when he behaved like an actor, graciously acknowledging the curtain calls, almost putting on special little acts for the populace. Television programmes brought his name, appearance and performances to hundreds of thousands of people who had never been, would never go, to a race-course in their lives.

Then disaster struck. On 27 December 1966, Arkle ran at Kempton in the King George VI steeplechase. For much of the race he led, though he was not jumping his best. At the last fence, Arkle jumped askew. He had botched a jump at other times in his career, but had always seemed to straighten out and come roaring on. This time he did not. Instead of the last brilliant dash that seemed so often to leave his opponents almost standing as it had at Navan at the beginning of his meteoric career, Arkle was struggling. He was game enough, but Dormant passed him and came in first.

The news crept round the course, was given out by radio and television, almost as though it were a national disaster. Arkle was crippled. The wonder horse was finished. He had, in fact, cracked a small bone inside his hoof, probably earlier in the race when he had hit a guard rail. He had showed his mettle and courage to the last, with pain and discomfort increasing all the time. It might be said that he had won another race even though he was not first over the line.

For a time he was kept at Kempton, with the box next to him overflowing with gifts from all over the world, and the post office kept busy delivering letters and telegrams. The day he eventually left again for Ireland was like the progress of a medieval monarch.

Many would say that all this public acclaim and sympathy was entirely ill-judged, sentimental and misplaced.

It may be so. But the horse has had a long and proud place in the story of man, sharing his triumphs and disasters, labouring for him, sporting with him, conquering with him, dying with him. No beast has done more in terms of toil and hardihood, courage and good faith.

Small wonder that the horse was an ancient symbol of kingship. Small wonder that people can sometimes still look to a horse almost as to a king. The oldest horse in Britain, nearly 400 feet long, was reputedly cut in the chalk of the Berkshire Downs by order of a king to celebrate his victory over the Danes.

The Uffington White Horse, cut into the Berkshire Downs

It may well be much older; and, high on the downland, it may stand as a symbol for everything the horse has meant to man in the long upward climb since the far-off days when, in the words of the historian G. M. Trevelyan, our ancestors, 'stone axe in hand, moved furtively ... ignorant that they lived upon an island, not dreaming that there could be other parts of the world besides this damp green woodland with its meres and marshes, wherein they hunted, a terror to its four-footed inhabitants and themselves afraid.'

All Sorts and Conditions

'*Knowing nothing of the cause . . . filled*
only with faith, love, and loyalty.'
– R.S.P.C.A. Memorial

Introduction

Though some horses have been pampered and kept almost entirely as show-pieces, the great majority through the centuries have earned their keep by working.

For practical purposes horses can be divided into three main groups. First there are the great draught horses, used for hauling the heaviest loads and weighing a ton or more. Next come the harness horses often, too, of considerable weight and strength, but combining power with style and greater speed. Many of them, such as the Hackney and the Yorkshire Coach, were in demand for pulling stage-coaches before the coming of the railway and the motor-car. The hackney was also much used as a smart carriage-horse. In America, a lighter, speedier type, known as the American Standard Breed, was developed from the English thoroughbred stock. Other famous breeds of harness horse are the Cleveland Bay, the Hanoverian and the Oldenburg.

The third main category are the saddle horses, i.e., those not normally used for pulling, but bred or trained to the saddle and to carry human beings. Often, of course, they are hardly to be distinguished in appearance or breeding from the harness horses. They are a type rather than a special breed. Many are thoroughbred or have a strong strain of thoroughbred blood. Much is expected of a good saddle horse. He should be able to show a fair turn of speed. He may not be beautiful to look at, but he must have stamina and powers of endurance enough to carry his rider for many hours through difficult conditions. The good hunter is such a type and, in days when the horse was much used in war, most of the cavalry rode horses of hunter stock.

A Clydesdale stallion

A Percheron cart stallion

Of all the working horses, none are more impressive or more lovable than the tallest and strongest of them all, the mighty draught breeds, chief among them the Belgian, the Clydesdale, the Percheron, the Shire, and the Suffolk or Suffolk Punch.

The Belgian or Flemish horse was a favourite battle-charger in medieval times. His descendant often stands as high as seventeen hands, with a compact muscular body and steep shoulders. Bay and chestnut are common colours.

Clydesdales came originally from Lanarkshire and are the result of cross-breeding of local horses with fine types from outside, often Shires or Flemish stock. They are more gracefully built than some, with arched necks and longer legs, but are still immensely strong. Though they can be of any colour, browns predominate. Patriotic Scotsmen swear by the Clydes. One of them, Will Ogilvie, wrote:

A Shire mare

A Suffolk mare

The Suffolk Punch will keep the road;
*   The Percheron goes gay;*
The Shire will lean against his load
*   All through the longest day;*
But where the ploughland meets the heather
*   And earth from sky divides,*
Through the misty Northern weather,
Stepping two and two together,
All fire and feather,
*   Come the Clydes!*

The Percheron came from La Perche, a district of France, bounded by Normandy to the north and west, which has always been famous for stock-rearing and farming. It was bred from heavy Flemish stock but crossed with more refined and lighter Arab blood, so that it tends to be more shapely and smaller than the other draught breeds. The commonest colour is grey.

The Shires are among the mightiest of them all and were formerly the chief farm-horses of England, descended from the early English Great Horse and bred by kings and nobles to carry them in full armour. With their powerful quarters, wide and deep body and characteristic thick hair on the legs, they were for long a favourite sight in the English countryside though, sadly enough, they are a rare survival in modern days of mechanization.

Some of the places where these great working horses can still be seen are the stables maintained by a number of leading brewing firms. It would doubtless be quicker and more economical to do away with them and rely on mechanical transport; but, mercifully, other counsels have so far prevailed, so that the old equestrian pride of England can still be seen, effortlessly pulling their heavy loads.

Some were exported to India in the nineteenth century, and were held in great respect by the native rulers, who called them 'the English elephants'.

13
Black Bess

c. A.D. 1730

Perhaps there is a lawless streak in all of us that makes us regard certain types of adventurer with a sort of admiration. Few people would care to boast that they had a murderer or traitor for an ancestor; but most would cheerfully acknowledge a pirate or buccaneer, though they were a sorry bunch of crooks on the whole, with little of loyalty, courage and skill among them.

The same is true of highwaymen. Since they were rebels against authority and were fond of telling tall stories about their own masterly exploits, they occupy a special niche in the affections of law-abiding people, along with other types of outlaw. Certainly they were capable at times of actions calculated to win the applause of the crowd and the sighs of fair ladies. When Jerry Abershaw, a young thug who terrorized the roads between London, Kingston and Wimbledon for some years at the end of the eighteenth century, was hanged on Kennington Common at the age of twenty-two, he went to the gallows with a rose between his lips.

When Claude Duval, more than a century before, found a lady good-looking enough in the coach he had held up, he would invite her to step down on the heath and dance a coranto with him. 'They danced,' says his biographer, 'and here it was that Du Vall performed marvels; the best master in London, except those that are French, was not able to shew footing as he did in his great French riding boots.'

His gallantry and nimbleness of foot did not, of course, prevent him from looting his victims; neither did it save him from being executed as a common crook, which he undoubtedly was, in 1670.

The best-known highwayman in English history is probably Dick Turpin, though there was little about him to distinguish him from fifty others of his profession. It was the horse and Harrison Ainsworth that did it.

Ainsworth was a solicitor-in-training who turned to the publishing and writing of books. In 1834 appeared the very successful novel *Rookwood*, and he followed it up with some thirty-eight more, most of them purporting to be historical, though Ainsworth cheerfully bent his history as much as he found necessary to fit his vivid energetic stories, that go along at a rare pace and are still readable.

Rookwood is one of the chief reasons that the story of Dick Turpin and Black Bess is so well known. But the sad thing is that Turpin never made the famous ride to York, on Black Bess or any other steed. The exploit related by Ainsworth was performed by another highwayman, John Nevison, who was born nearly seventy years before Turpin and was hanged at York in 1684.

About six years before, Nevison had robbed a traveller near Rochester in Kent at four o'clock in the morning. He was afraid that a witness had recognized him and therefore decided to provide himself with an alibi that no court could question. Riding like the wind, he crossed the Thames at Tilbury and stormed up the Great North Road to York. There were plenty of friends and acquaintances on the way to supply him with fresh horses. Time after time he left one blown and lathered mount behind and leapt on the back of another. At 7.45 that evening he was more than 230 miles away from the scene of his crime and in the eminently respectable company of the Lord Mayor of York on the bowling green at York.

There had been more spectacular rides; but, as a matter of sober fact, no rider could have accomplished the distance on a single horse, as Turpin and Black Bess are traditionally supposed to have done in the time. Nevison's alibi was good enough when they arrested him later for the Kent robbery, and he was released. He was so pleased with himself that he boasted about his ride and was arrested again and sentenced to the gallows. It is said that Charles II himself, who always liked a good story and a bold rogue, intervened and pardoned him, christening the highwayman 'Swift Nicks'.

But Nevison's ride to York does not leave Dick Turpin horseless. Turpin undoubtedly had a mare of great quality, since Black Bess was being talked about and sung about a long time before Harrison Ainsworth wrote *Rookwood*.

Turpin was born near Saffron Walden in Essex, the son of an innkeeper. He was apprenticed to a butcher, but soon fell into evil company and joined up with a gang of thieves who specialized in deer-stealing and smuggling.

Having served his apprenticeship to crime, Turpin took to the road and went into partnership with a well-known highwayman named Tom King. They made a formidable pair and ranged widely in the south of England, making a fearsome reputation for themselves. Tom King at least escaped hanging; for in a confused struggle when the law had caught up with the couple on one occasion, he was accidentally killed by a shot from Turpin.

This is fact. But it was at this point that Harrison Ainsworth transferred the Nevison story to Dick Turpin and sent the latter galloping from Kilburn to York.

It was true enough that Turpin went to Yorkshire after the struggle in which his partner had been accidentally killed. For a time he played the role of a country gentleman, accepted in sporting circles and joining in the social life of the district. But retribution was not far away. He was convicted of horse-stealing at York and hanged there on 7 April 1739.

What was Black Bess like? According to Harrison Ainsworth:

In colour she was perfectly black, with a skin smooth on the surface as polished jet; not a single white hair could be detected in her satin coat. In make she was magnificent. Every point was perfect, beautiful, compact; modelled, in little, for strength and speed. Arched was her neck as that of a swan; clean and fine were her lower limbs, as those of the gazelle; round and sound as a drum was her carcass, and as broad as a cloth-yard shaft her width of chest.

'"Shout for your lives," cried Patterson, "the turnpike man will hear us – the gate is shut." Dick coolly calculated its height, spoke a few words to Bess, gently patted her neck – stuck spurs into her sides, and cleared the spikes by an inch.' The legend of Dick Turpin's ride from a contemporary print.

It may have been so. It would not have been the first time, nor will it be the last, that a horse was of better stuff than its master.

14
Spanker

c. A.D. 1820

Spanker's name and reputation survive only in the notice of an auction sale held at Epsom in 1820. It is of interest, not only for the alliterative ingenuity of the writer of the advertisement, but for its remarkable vocabulary, some of which is of considerable antiquity and interesting origin. 'Spavin', for example, comes from an early word for 'sparrow' and is used of a horse which, because of a bony enlargement in the hock joint, lifts his leg like a sparrow or sparrow-hawk; and 'surbate' is from the old French *solbatu* or 'bruised foot'.

On Saturday next will be sold by auction the strong, staunch, sturdy, stout, sound, safe, sinewy, serviceable, strapping, swift, smart, sightly, sprightly, spirited, sure-footed, well-sized, well-shaped, sorrell steed of superlative symmetry, styled Spanker, with small star and snip – free from strain, spavin, string-halt, stranguary, staggers, scouring, strangles, sallenders, surfeit, starfoot, splint, scabs, scars, sores, shambling gait. He is neither spur-galled, sinew-shrunk, saddle-galled, shell-toothed, sling-gutted, surbated, short-winded, or shoulder-slipped, and is sound in the swordpoint and stifle joint. Has neither sitfast, snaggle-teeth, sandcrack, staring coat, swelled sheath, nor scattered hoofs, nor is he sour, sulky, stubborn, or sullen in temper; never slips, trips, stalks, starts, stops, shakes, snarvels, stumbles, or stocks in the stable. Has a showy, stylish, switch tail.

15
Comanche Charley

c. A.D. 1835

George Catlin, born in 1796 in Pennsylvania, devoted much of his life to recording the life and customs of the American Indians who, under ever increasing white pressure, were being driven from their haunts and hunting grounds and were in danger of extinction.

He was a skilled artist and was able to make thousands of sketches and paintings of these vanishing peoples, both in North and South America. Much of his work is now in a special Catlin Gallery in the National Museum, Washington. Catlin was not content merely to go on tour of the native territories. He lived with the Indians and learned their languages. In 1841 he published two plentifully illustrated books called *The Manners, Customs and Conditions of the North American Indians*.

The horse was much prized by the Indians, not only for the purpose of making war but as a means of livelihood in pursuit of the buffalo and bison on which they relied for hides and food. Special hunting parties were formed for the chase and capture of wild horses, and the braves were ready to travel great distances and endure acute hardships to acquire their mounts. One writer records that 'to steal the horse of an adverse tribe is considered as an exploit almost as heroic as the killing of an enemy'.

Among the North American Indians, the Comanches seem to have been among the most far-roving in their hunting and fighting and to have produced the most brilliant horsemen. Catlin recorded an extraordinary feat that the warriors learnt for the purpose of battle. When they passed an enemy they would drop down on the far side of the horse, with only a heel on the horse's back. In this position, galloping at full speed, the Indian brave still kept control of shield, bow and arrows and fourteen-foot lance. He would shoot over the horse's back or under his neck and, if necessary, whirl over and drop to the other side in a moment.

The Comanches managed this trick riding with the aid of a special hair halter which hung in a loop under the horse's neck. When the rider dropped, he thrust his elbow into the loop and, with his heel left over the back of the horse, had enough support to stay with it and to swing himself upright again when he wished.

The horses were often as clever as the riders. George Catlin himself rode a Comanche horse brought in from the wild, christened it Charley and became very attached to it.

When he was travelling from settlement to settlement, Catlin usually camped by some little stream, where he picketed Charley, leaving him tethered but free to browse over a fair-sized circle. One night Charley contrived to slip his lasso and wandered off in great enjoyment of his freedom.

George Catlin's drawing of himself and Charley.

Catlin picked up the lasso and went in pursuit, talking as winningly as he knew how. But Charley was more than a match for him, daintily eluding the rope and refusing to be cajoled back. At last, as darkness fell, Catlin gave up, came back to camp and threw himself down to sleep in a very bad temper, thinking that he would have to finish his trip on foot.

In the middle of the night, lying on his back, he was awakened by a stealthy movement. Peering up through half-closed eye-lids he saw to his horror a huge figure looming over him. His first thought was that a hostile Indian had crept up on him and was about to scalp him. For a moment he was frozen with fright as he waited for the tomahawk to descend on his helpless head.

Then he suddenly realized it was Charley. The horse had eaten his fill and had returned to his master, standing stock still with his head over the sleeping figure. Catlin contentedly went back to his dreams.

When he awoke with the daylight, Charley had given up sentry duty and had taken himself off to breakfast at the creek. Once more Catlin took his lasso and set off in pursuit; and once more Charley swerved and curvetted, always just out of reach.

With the memory of that figure gently standing over him in the night, obviously out of affection and fondness for his companionship, Catlin tried another scheme. Completely ignoring Charley, he came back to his small fire, packed up his few belongings and set off along the trail, rifle in hand and the saddle on his back.

After a while, Catlin stopped and looked back. Charley had left his breakfast and was standing looking first at the deserted camp and then at the man disappearing up the trail. Apparently realizing that the game was over and that his master had really left, Charley gave an indignant neigh, took to his heels and raced past Catlin, then stopped on the path ahead and waited.

This time he patiently dropped his head as George Catlin put on the bridle and saddle. Then, happy in surrender, he tossed his handsome head and the two went on their way.

16
The Taming of Cruiser

A.D. 1858

'His name will take rank among the great social reformers of the nineteenth century.'

So wrote a contributor to the *Illustrated London News* in the 1850s. It was a strong claim to make in a century that had seen the work of such people as William Wilberforce, who laboured to free slaves; Elizabeth Fry, who devoted her energies to prison reform; and Lord Shaftesbury, who achieved so much in the cause of factory workers and chimney sweeps.

The odd thing is that the man thus acclaimed was a horse-tamer named Rarey, a fair-haired, light-footed, grey-eyed farmer from Ohio in the United States, who took London by storm in the year 1858 and had the greatest horsemen and members of the noblest families, both men and women, queueing to learn from him.

Rarey had been a horse-breaker from his early youth. At first he tried the old bronco-busting, rough-riding methods and 'in the course of his adventures broke almost every bone in his body, for his pluck was greater than his science.' It seemed to him that there must be better methods of taming these spirited horses and he talked with everyone he thought might hold the secret – cow-hands, wandering horsemen, circus trainers; and he read every book on the subject he could lay his hands on.

The result, allied to an obvious natural gift for handling horses, was a set of principles that he put into practice with great effect in Ohio and Texas, teaching for a modest fee and unknown outside a limited area.

Looking back, it may seem extraordinary that Rarey's system

should have been such a great innovation and, eventually, should bring him fame and fortune. It was based on a simple creed that gentleness and fearlessness on the part of the horsemen, allied to the use of certain simple equipment, could tame the most wild and vicious horse and make him a useful member of society. The three fundamental principles he set out were:

First – that he [the horse] is so constituted by nature that he will not offer resistance to any demand made of him which he fully comprehends, if made in a way consistent with the laws of his nature.

Second – that he has no consciousness of his strength beyond his experience, and can be handled according to our will without force.

Third – that we can, in compliance with the laws of his nature, by which he examines all things new to him, take any object, however frightful, around, over, or on him, that does not inflict pain – without causing him to fear.

In the course of his work as a horse-tamer, Mr Rarey met a sharp-witted businessman named Goodenough, whose shrewd eye saw something of much more than local appeal about the farmer and his skill with horses. He proposed a business partnership with him and set about showing him off to the right people. In Canada, Goodenough managed to ensure that General Sir William Eyre, Commander-in-Chief of the British forces, should see Rarey at work. Sir William was so impressed that he gave the pair letters of introduction to the Horse Guards in England and to several influential families.

Rarey and Goodenough arrived in London and, encouraged by the support they received as a result of Sir William Eyre's letters, opened a subscription list for pupils wishing to learn Rarey's system of horse-taming. The fee was £10 10s each, and the lessons would not begin till five hundred pupils had been enrolled.

While he was waiting for the list to fill up, Rarey crossed over to Paris to show his skill with a vicious and half-mad horse named Stafford. For a whole year Stafford had refused to let anyone groom him and was kept in close confinement in his box. Given the least chance he attacked anyone who came near him with threshing fore-feet and bared teeth. He had been blindfolded, muzzled, hobbled, in efforts to subdue him. Nothing had the least effect and he was about to be destroyed.

Here was a stiff enough challenge to Rarey's fanciful theories, and a great crowd of horse experts assembled in Paris to see the result of the contest *Stafford v. Rarey*. One can do no better than quote the report from the *Paris Illustrated Journal*:

After being alone with Stafford for an hour and a half, Mr Rarey rode on him into the Riding School, guiding him with a common snaffle-bridle. The appearance of the horse was completely altered: he was calm and docile. His docility did not seem to be produced by fear or constraint, but the result of perfect confidence. The astonishment of the spectators was increased when Mr Rarey unbridled him, and guided the late savage animal, with a mere motion of his hands or indication with his leg, as easily as a trained circus-horse. Then, dashing into a gallop, he stopped him short with a single word.

Mr Rarey concluded his first exhibition by beating a drum on Stafford's back, and passing his hand over his head and mouth. Stafford was afterwards ridden by a groom, and showed the same docility in his hands as those of Mr Rarey.

Mr Rarey succeeded at his first attempt in putting him in harness with a mare, although he had never had his head through a collar before; and he went as quietly as the best-broken carriage-horse in Paris.

Rarey came back to England to face another challenge, just as formidable. This was to tame the horse who was reckoned to be the most vicious stallion in England, one 'who could do more fighting in less time than any horse in the world.'

Cruiser, who belonged to Lord Dorchester, had been a Derby favourite, but had broken down before the race, and his trainer was delighted to send him back to his owner. The *Morning Post* of 2 March 1858 reported:

When started for Rawcliffe, he told the man who led him on no account to put him into a stable, as he would never get him out. This injunction was of course disregarded, for when the man wanted some refreshment, he put him into a country public-house stable, and left him, and to get him out, the roof of the building had to be pulled off. At Rawcliffe, he was always exhibited by a groom with a ... bludgeon in his hand, and few were bold enough to venture into his yard. This animal, whose temper has depreciated him perhaps a thousand pounds in value, would be 'the right horse in the right place' for Mr Rarey.

Mr Rarey obliged. On 7 April, Lord Dorchester reported that he:

... took Cruiser in hand, and in three hours Mr Rarey and myself mounted him. He had not been ridden for nearly three years, and was so vicious that it was impossible even to dress him, and it was necessary to keep him muzzled constantly. The following morning Mr Rarey led him behind an open carriage, on his road to London. This horse was returned to me ... on account of his vice, it being considered as much as a man's life was worth to attend to him.

Some account of Rarey's work on Cruiser has survived. He had already secured him and taken him forty miles behind a dog-cart to steady and tire him. Many men would have reckoned that enough for one day. But perseverance and matchless patience were two of Rarey's greatest qualities. That same night, in the quiet of Cruiser's stable, with thick straw for the horse to fall on, he 'set to work ... to tame him limb by limb, and inch by inch, and from that day until he produced him in public, he never missed a day without spending twice a day from two to three hours with him.'

Cruiser was first made helpless by a gag-bit, non-cutting straps and hobbles. Then Rarey 'gentled' him, caressing him and talking softly. Then he forced him to lie down, 'caressing him again, stroking him again, stroking every limb, talking to him in soothing tones.'

If the horse attempted any show of viciousness, the spectators saw the strange sight of Rarey lifting the great helpless head, shaking it and scolding Cruiser as though he were a naughty child. Temper calmed, off would come the gag-bit, with the reward of a drink of

cool water and a handful of fragrant hay. Then up, and a short ride, the horse being checked at a word.

The taming of Cruiser brought Rarey a comfortable income. When the public learnt that he had brought the horse to London the day after 'he first backed him and had ridden him within three hours after the first interview', they clamoured to fill up his subscription list for the ten guineas lessons.

He made his headquarters in Kinnerton Street, just off Belgrave Square, and there Cruiser, his head high and his pride unbroken, but obedient to the least word of the Ohio farmer who had conquered him with kindness, was shown to the admiring crowd. Long before the doors of the riding school were open, the little street was crowded with a strange procession of people, the noble and the fashionable, the rich and famous, along with the humble and poor, all come to see a man with a horse; those who could afford it thrusting their guineas into the hands of a bewildered secretary at the door, in order to make sure of their lessons.

Rarey's reputation was such that he was engaged to teach cavalry officers and army riding masters; he lectured to London cabmen on the treatment of their horses, and even imparted his secrets to the Prime Minister, Lord Palmerston.

With fees, subscriptions and the profits of a small book he published on his methods, Mr Rarey and his astute business partner are estimated to have made some £20,000. Not many men have deserved a fortune more than Rarey, for his system of 'rendering horses docile and affectionate, fit for hacks or chargers, ladies' pads or harness, or the safe conveyance of the aged, crippled, and sick.'

Perhaps, after all, a man who saved countless horses from bludgeoning, beating, starving, blinding and destruction, in the effort to break them, is fit company for the other great reformers of his time.

17
The Black Horse of Kasala

A.D. 1875–76

In the long history of the saddle-horse, there is no episode more remarkable than Burnaby's ride to Khiva and back.

Captain Fred Burnaby of the Royal Horse Guards was a large
man, weighing fifteen or sixteen stone. He was the son of a clergyman, but showed little inclination to follow his father's footsteps and
live out his life quietly in some country parish. He had, from his
earliest years, what his old nurse used to call a 'contradictorious'
spirit. This led him, sometimes with unfortunate results, to rebel
against authority and to take an opposite line of thought to everyone
else.

He was also born with a hunger for adventure and far horizons.
When he was seventeen he joined the Royal Horse Guards and during the next fifteen years managed to travel in Central and Southern
America, Spain, Morocco, Russia and Egypt. In February 1875 he
was in Khartoum, having just returned from a visit to the British
army on the White Nile.

England was in the grip of winter; but in Khartoum Captain
Burnaby was lounging on the window-sill in stifling heat, glancing at
an old newspaper from home. In the room a number of men of
different nationalities were arguing and gossiping. One of them said:

'I wonder where we shall be this time next year?'

Burnaby's eye, wandering over the old newspaper, suddenly saw
a paragraph saying that the Russian Government in St Petersburg
had issued orders that no foreigner was to be allowed to travel in
Russian Asia. In fact, an Englishman who had just attempted an
expedition had already been turned back.

This was just the sort of thing to rouse Burnaby's 'contradictor-iousness'. He had some leave due to him and he determined to fulfil an old ambition, to travel through Central Asia, much of it in Russian occupation, to the ancient town and kingdom of Khiva, which today is part of the Socialist Soviet Republic of Uzbekistan. Khiva has a very long history. It was conquered by Persians, by Arabs and Turks. In the seventeenth century the hard-riding Cossack cavalry plundered it. Peter the Great, hearing of gold deposits in the River Oxus, sent an army there. The old city was a place of lofty domes and slender, painted minarets set about by a double wall of brick and clay, in parts fifty feet high, and pierced only by four great wooden gates reinforced with iron. Surrounding it were miles of orchard and avenues of mulberry trees. In the centre of the city was the great palace of the Khan, or ruler, its richly ornamented pillars and coloured tiles gleaming in the sunlight, its entrances guarded by warriors armed with great curving scimitars, coloured sashes round their silken uniforms, their weather-beaten faces crowned with tall fur hats.

A journey to Khiva was not something to be contemplated lightly. It would involve a journey on horseback through some of the most bitter and hostile country in the world, in mid-winter. Describing it later, Burnaby wrote:

The cold of the Kirghiz desert is a thing unknown I believe in any other part of the world, or even in the Arctic regions. An enormous expanse of flat country, extending for hundreds of miles, and devoid of everything save snow and salt lakes ... would have to be traversed ... The winds in those parts of Asia are unknown to the inhabitants of Europe. When they grumble at the so-called east wind, they can little imagine what the wind is like in those countries which lie exposed to the full fury of its first onslaught. For there you meet with no warm ocean to mollify its rigour, no trees, no rising land, no hills or mountains to check it in its course. It blows on uninterrup-tedly over a vast snow- and salt-covered track ... The sensation is more like the application of the edge of a razor than anything else to which it can be compared.

98

Undaunted by the prospect of such conditions, Captain Burnaby, after his return to England, made his preparations for his ride to Khiva. His wardrobe soon contained numerous thick jerseys, flannel shirts and outside garments of furs and skins. Helped by the advice of an Arctic traveller, he had made a great sleeping bag of waterproofed sail-cloth, ten feet round and seven and a half feet long. It was a wonderful bag, but Burnaby was to find that it was 'of great convenience for every purpose save the one for which it was originally intended.'

The manufacturer (and perhaps Burnaby himself) had not realized how large a hole he would need to get into the bag. A bulky man to start with, his proportions became alarming when he was enveloped in several layers of thick clothing topped by furs; so that, when he attempted to dive into his comfortable sleeping quarters he got badly stuck and had to devise some other means of sleeping. But at last all his preparations were complete and on 30 November 1875, the great adventure began, prosaically enough by cab and by train from Victoria Station to Dover. Six weeks later, with the first part of the journey completed, he was in Kasala and set about purchasing a horse for the arduous ride of close on 500 miles to distant Khiva. When the news got around Kasala that the Englishman was looking for a mount for which he was prepared to pay well, an extraordinary procession appeared. In Burnaby's words, this was composed of:

excited natives, looking, many of them, like animated bundles of rags, so thickly were they enveloped in shreds and tatters. Each ... was astride on some sort of quadruped – camels, horses, donkeys, all were brought on the scene, forming a comical picture which will never be effaced from my memory.

The horses were, for the most part, of the worst description; that is to say, so far as appearance was concerned. Their ribs in many instances almost protruded through the skin, the proprietors of the quadrupeds having apparently been engaged in solving the knotty point as to how near they could reduce them to a straw-a-day diet without their animals succumbing to the experiment ... Except for their excessive leanness they looked more like huge Newfoundland dogs ... and had been turned out in the depth of winter with no other covering save the thick coats which nature had given them.

From this motley assemblage Captain Burnaby at length selected a little black horse. The prospect of the animal surviving the long and gruelling journey to Khiva seemed remote in the extreme. He looked tough, but was only about fourteen hands high, compared with the much taller and heavier English horses to which Burnaby was accustomed. The most impressive thing about him was his saddle, a brightly painted affair, gilded and enamelled, and with 'a small knob about six inches long, sticking up at the pommel' which 'looked especially contrived for the impalement of the rider'. Burnaby bought horse, saddle and bridle for £5, a price considered high in Kasala.

On 12 January 1876 the cavalcade of camels and ragamuffin horses set out from Kasala. The sentries outside the Governor's

house stuffed their overshoes with hay and ran backwards and forwards non-stop to stop their feet freezing. Moustaches froze into
blocks of solid ice.

The enormous figure of Captain Burnaby, encased in layers of
clothes and sheepskins, lumbered towards his little black mount,
watched by his retinue. To add to the pony's burdens he was laden
with huge stirrup irons. After a great deal of puffing and heaving,
Burnaby struggled into the saddle. The black horse visibly sank a
little and was heard to groan. He was, after all, carrying a total
weight of about 20 stone. A little Tartar servant, perched on a sack
of corn on top of a camel, prophesied that the horse would soon break
down and they would all be able to feast off him.

Before long they were in what looked like an infinite waste of white.
Gales lashed round them, blinding their eyes and piling the snow
in thick ridges, through which the animals struggled gamely, their

eyes, like their riders', encrusted with frozen tears. They crossed great frozen rivers, gleaming beneath the sun like burnished metal, passed salt lakes, threaded their way through mountain passes. Often Burnaby dozed in the saddle, only waking when the little black horse lurched sideways beneath his sagging load. At intervals they camped and slept more soundly, warmed by blazing fires of brushwood and bramble.

After 300 miles Burnaby's mount, far from being ready for the cooking-pot, was as spry as ever. He still looked like a furry skeleton but was evidently appreciating the barley he was given to eat in place of grass.

The little black horse went on; on, with the snow now thinning and sand becoming more visible beneath it, 'beneath the influence of a glaring sun, like a sea of molten gold studded with silver isles'; on through a great mountain barrier where the gleaming quartz dazzled the eyes of the travellers and where rain rushed down in foaming channels to join the River Oxus; on through the pass to a vast level plain, irrigated with canals and dotted with villages and with a few tall trees, the first the expedition had seen since leaving Kasala hundreds of miles back.

Burnaby was now within easy distance of Khiva, his destination. But there were still obstacles to be overcome. He could not even enter the city without writing to the Khan to seek permission. Indeed, the District Governor of Kasala had warned him that, if he went without an escort, the Khan would probably have his eyes put out or throw him into a dungeon. This was a problem, since the letter would have to be written in the Tartar language and no one in the party knew enough of it to put the request into suitably courteous and flattering words.

Fortunately, in one of the villages where they were entertained as guests, there was a *moullah*, or learned man, who, said the guide, 'could write beautiful things, so soft and sweet that they were like the sounds of sheep bleating in the distance'.

The *moullah*, equipped with a bullock's horn inkstand and a long pen made of cane, indeed wrote a flowery and beautiful letter; but insisted on calling Burnaby a *polkovnik* (colonel) instead of *kapitan* (captain) because, he said, a mere captain would be looked down on in Khiva. In the end, Burnaby wrote his own letter, in Russian, simply saying 'An English gentleman who is travelling through Central Asia requests the permission of his Majesty the Khan to visit his celebrated capital'.

The messenger was dispatched and Burnaby hopefully continued his journey towards the capital. When he was within a few hours' ride of Khiva he decided that he had better remove a thirteen-day growth of beard and enter the city respectably clean shaven. The Khivans wanted him to keep his beard but shave his head, as they did; but Burnaby decided this would not suit him.

By this time the whole town had apparently heard that a strange Englishman was within the walls and was about to be shaved. The street and barber's shop were crowded with sightseers anxious to see the performance. They were highly delighted when the blunt razor, used without any soap, hacked away at the thick beard and made Burnaby wince with pain. They had not hoped for such delightful entertainment, and their mirth became almost hysterical when the barber, becoming nervous, slightly gashed the Englishman's cheek.

But at last the fun was over and, after being entertained to a meal, Captain Burnaby mounted his horse and continued his journey, soon to be met by two Khivan noblemen, who had been sent by the Khan to escort the travellers into the city.

Of Captain Burnaby's reception by the great Khan and his entertainment there and in the surrounding countryside, there is no space to tell here. This is, after all, the story of a horse. Burnaby eventually received a telegram from H.R.H. the Duke of Cambridge, Field-Marshal Commander-in-Chief of the British army, ordering his far-travelled officer to return at once to European Russia. This was a command that could not be disobeyed. Burnaby had given his horse nine days' rest. Now once more he took on his twenty-stone burden and, game as ever, began the long ride back to Kasala whence he had started.

This time the going was faster; indeed, when the horses neared Kasala they raced over the last few miles as though scenting home. Burnaby and some of his companions reached the town at midday on 12 February, having ridden the final 371 miles in nine days and two hours, averaging more than 40 miles a day through difficult country. Previously, the black horse had carried him nearly 500 miles. In spite of it all, Burnaby said, 'he had never been either sick or lame during the journey, and had galloped the last seventeen miles through the snow to Kasala in one hour and twenty-five minutes'.

And the end of it all?

It was no honourable retirement and a comfortable stable. The black horse had simply done a job. The job was finished and others remained to be done. Burnaby had bought him for forty roubles – about five pounds. He sold him in Kasala for three pounds ten shillings.

As he said, he had no reason to complain of his bargain.

18
Gato and Mancha
A.D. 1925–1928

'I rode some 10,000 miles in two and a half years.'

This terse statement by Aimé Felix Tschiffely, a Swiss-born school-master, summarized one of the greatest feats of sustained endurance of modern times. Indeed, it would be difficult to find any sort of parallel since Marco Polo made his way overland to China, through the peaks of the Pamirs and the arid Gobi desert nearly 700 years ago.

Yet, when he came to write the story, Tschiffely regarded it, not so much as a personal achievement, as the tale of two horses.

He was about thirty years old when, in 1925, an idea that had been shaping in his head for several years became a definite decision and was translated into action – to go on horseback from Buenos Aires, in Argentina, to New York. Put baldly like that, in an age when men can confidently journey to the moon and back, the project sounds nothing very remarkable. But one must consider what it meant – 10,000 miles through extremes of cold and heat; a route through every conceivable type of countryside and terrain, including bleak mountain passes, dense forests, steaming swamps and lifeless deserts; uncertain food and water supplies; threats from hostile Indians, snakes and poisonous insects; the danger of accident, disease and sickness far from any hope of medical help; and, perhaps above all, the doubt whether any horses, however hardy, could be expected to stand up to the journey of 10,000 miles through such extremes and perils.

Nevertheless, undeterred by prophecies of disaster, Tschiffely went about his preparations. Clearly, the first essential was to find suitable horses, and here he was fortunate in meeting Doctor Emilio

Solanet, an authority on, and breeder of, Creole horses (Criollos), which have a great reputation for hard work, endurance and the ability to travel long distances.

In the year 1535 the Spanish general Pedro de Mendoza sailed up the River Plate and formed a settlement at a spot where now stands the city of Buenos Aires, capital and chief port of Argentina. The long and hazardous journey from Spain had meant that few horses could accompany the expedition. Those that did arrive, intended for the officers, were of fine Spanish breeding, with a mixture of Arab and Barbary blood.

At first the settlement was a failure and was overrun by hostile Indians. It seems likely that the Spanish horses and their descendants – the first horses to be seen in this part of the world – were not massacred with their owners but left free to wander and live as best they could off the countryside. Their fight for existence in the wild, the abrupt changes of temperature, the need to travel long distances in search of food and water, killed off the weakest and resulted in a strain of horse that was immensely strong and agile, still with the blood of high-bred ancestors in their veins, but now capable of greater endurance under all conditions.

This was the type of horse that Doctor Solanet recommended to Tschiffely as companions for his proposed journey, and it happened that he had two ready at hand, still only partly broken in. They were fifteen and sixteen years of age and had belonged to a Patagonian Indian chief named Liempichun. The fifteen year old was coffee-coloured and called Gato (from the Spanish meaning 'cat'). The other, Mancha, was red, with large splashes of white – what in England would be called a piebald and in the United States a pinto (from the Spanish word meaning spotted or mottled). It is a strange fact that in some parts of South America piebalds are unknown, with the result that, for example in Columbia, other horses shied at the sight of Mancha, one even bolting with his rider when Tschiffely appeared round a bend.

There was nothing beautiful about the two animals, except perhaps their bright, lively eyes. They were sturdy, thick-necked and not very graceful in movement. But they were tough, agile and spirited. To join Doctor Solanet's *estancia* (ranch or country estate) they had made a journey of more than a thousand miles, living off whatever they could find for themselves in the sparse countryside. Indeed, so accustomed were they to hard fare that for some time they would not touch the richer foods, including barley and oats, which Tschiffely provided, preferring to devour the coarse straw put down for their bedding when they were stabled.

To summarize adequately the incidents of that journey of nearly three years would be a near-impossible task. It is better to read the traveller's own account in his book *Tschiffely's Ride*, unpretentious in style but packed with incident and information. He himself reflected that, over all that long and hazardous trail, beset with every imaginable sort of danger, 'of high adventures, hair-breadth escapes, and deeds of daring, there were few.' But that is too modest an assessment.

On one occasion, when they were crossing a ford haunted by an enormous crocodile which had been known to attack men and mules, an extra pack-horse Tschiffely was using took fright and sent Mancha and his rider tumbling down off the ten-foot high bank into the water. Though they were completely submerged, with Tschiffely underneath, he managed to hold on and got his mount back to dry land before the crocodile made his appearance.

Another day, Gato fell into a deep canyon and, by the luckiest chance, had his fall checked by a tree growing straight out from the side. Tschiffely climbed down, fastened ropes round the horse and, with the help of some friendly Indians, hauled him back to the top.

One hazard was the necessity of sometimes crossing deep ravines and wild rivers crossed only by rickety structures of rope, wire and fibre which swayed alarmingly and sagged ominously in the middle. They are so frightening that people often have to be blindfolded and carried across on stretchers. How then did Mancha and Gato fare? This is how Tschiffely described one such crossing:

Spanning a wild river the bridge looked like a long, thin hammock swung high up from one rock to another ... the floor was made of sticks laid cross-wise and covered with some coarse fibre matting to give a foothold and to prevent slipping that would inevitably prove fatal. The width of this extra-ordinary piece of engineering was no more than four feet, and its length must have been roughly one hundred and fifty yards.

I went to examine it closely, and the very sight of it made me feel giddy, and the thought of what might easily happen produced a feeling in my stomach as if I had swallowed a block of ice ... I unsaddled the horses, and giving the Indian the lead-line, I made signs to him to go ahead with Mancha first. Knowing the horse well, I caught him by the tail and walked behind talking to him to keep him quiet. When we stepped on the bridge he hesitated for a moment, then he sniffed the matting with suspicion, and after examining the strange surroundings he listened to me and cautiously advanced. As we approached the deep sag in the middle, the bridge began to sway horribly, and for a moment I was afraid the horse would try to turn back, which would have been the end of him; but no, he had merely stopped to wait until the swinging motion was less, and then he moved on again ... Once we started upwards after having crossed the middle, even the horse seemed to realize that we had passed the worst part, for he now began to hurry towards safety. His weight shook the bridge so much that I had to catch hold of the wires on the sides to keep my balance. Gato, when his turn came, seeing his companion on the other side, gave less trouble and crossed over as steadily as if he were walking along a trail.

On another occasion, Mancha's agility posed Tschiffely a pretty problem. Part of the trail had been swept away by a landslide, leaving a jagged gap between rocks and a drop of several hundred feet. To go back would mean a detour taking two or three days, but Tschiffely decided it was too risky to try to jump the gap and pre-pared to turn back. While he was adjusting Gato's pack, Mancha wandered casually up to the yawning gap in the trail, considered it a moment, then jumped. He landed safely on the other side and went on with his grazing.

Now Tschiffely was in a dilemma, with one horse on each side of

the chasm. To give himself time for thought, he tied Gato to a rock, then managed to jump the gap himself to do the same for Mancha, in case he decided to wander further. Tschiffely decided that there was nothing to be gained by bringing Mancha back. He returned to Gato, removed his saddle and pack, and brought him up to the chasm, which he jumped as neatly as a goat and rejoined Mancha. Then, crossing and recrossing several times, Tschiffely rigged up a rope and brought over the pack and saddle.

Such exploits Tschiffely apparently regarded neither as 'high adventures' nor 'deeds of daring', though most of us would regard them as such and talk about them for the rest of our lives.

When at last the great ride ended, with all the wiseacres who had denounced the expedition as impossible now discreetly silent, Tschiffely and his two companions were greeted as heroes in Washington and New York. In Washington, the adventurer was received by the President of the United States at the White House. Praise, celebrations, awards, banquets, filled the days and nights.

Gato and Mancha took it all very quietly, unless anyone tried to get too close or familiar. To the last, after the discipline of a ride of ten thousand miles, Mancha would allow no one but Tschiffely to saddle him.

What was to be done with them now it was all over? Many people wanted the horses put in some public park where they could always be seen by curious sightseers. But Tschiffely talked with Doctor Solanet again, and they came to the admirable decision that Gato and Mancha had earned a better fate than that. Instead, they were given their freedom on a ranch back in Argentina, with miles of rolling plains and pampas for their enjoyment.

To quote some words James Agate used of his best-loved horse, Tschiffely, Gato and Mancha 'had in overwhelming measure that supreme quality of man and horse – pluck.'

19
Great Men in Rotten Row

c. A.D. 1830

Rotten Row, in London, runs for nearly a mile through Kensington Gardens and Hyde Park, from Alexandra Gate to Hyde Park Corner. It has for a very long time been a favourite place in the City for the exercise of horses and as a fashionable parade, though the standard of riders and their mounts has not always been of the highest. A well-known writer on the horse, Samuel Sidney, said in 1873:

It is quite true that people who ought to know better ride horses in Rotten Row in the height of the season which are as much out of place in that scene of equestrian luxury as a coalheaver in the costume of his trade in the stalls of the opera. Some ride coach-horses of camel-like proportions; some ride brutes that would be useful in a carrier's cart and call them cobs . . . Tall men are to be seen on ponies, and short men on giraffes . . . . Ladies who have declined to go into a weighing machine, in spite of the tempting invitations at every metropolitan railway station, are to be seen risking their lives on screws two stone under their weight.

But Sidney also gave a serious and historically interesting picture of the Rotten Row he remembered when he was about eighteen years old and William IV had just come to the throne in 1830.

The King himself was no horseman and did not always stand on ceremony. The state coach at the time was drawn by eight gigantic cream horses and the royal stables also contained splendid teams of six black stallions, six white stallions and 'several sixes' of Yorkshire bays. All had to have their manes elaborately plaited, the creams with purple ribbons and the rest with crimson. When the King suddenly decided to drive to dissolve Parliament in 1831, the Master

George Cruikshank pokes fun at 'Tom and Jerry sporting their "bits of blood" among the Pinks of Rotten Row', early nineteenth century

of the Horse protested that there would be no time to plait the manes of the state carriage horses. He was horrified when the King said that, if they could not be got ready, he would go down to the House in a hackney coach – the equivalent of a modern taxi-cab.

In comparison with the rough-and-ready William – who was, after all, a sailor – his brother the Duke of Cumberland, who had served in both the English and Hanoverian armies and attained the rank of Field-Marshal, was 'a remarkable specimen of the stiff Hanoverian style of horsemanship'. Soon after 1815, a Prussian riding master was employed, with the direct encouragement of the Prince Regent, to teach the English cavalry to ride in a stiff straight-legged style with a long stirrup, in much the same manner that a mediæval knight rode in his heavy armour. It was an unnatural style and resulted in many casualties, so that this manner of horsemanship was soon dropped in favour of something more workmanlike and practical.

Another rider watched by Samuel Sidney on his first visit to Rotten Row was 'a ponderous man, with a pleasant good-humoured face, dressed in white cord breeches, top boots, with silk stockings seen between them, a blue coat with gilt buttons, a buff waistcoat, and a broad-rimmed hat.' Young Sidney thought this must be some wealthy farmer up from the country, still sticking to a style of dress that had been fashionable some twenty-five years before. But, to his surprise, he found it was no less a person than the Chancellor of the Exchequer, Lord Althorpe, known as 'Honest Jack.'

Althorpe was certainly a countryman, and Sidney could be forgiven for thinking him a farmer. Althorpe, in fact, would have taken it as a compliment, for he loved country pursuits better than anything and only became a politician from a sense of duty. He was that rare type, a really honest politician, trusted by his opponents as well as his friends.

'Not the sort for Rotten Row'—another nineteenth-century engraving

In the Rotten Row cavalcade was another remarkable figure – that of Count Alfred Guillaume Gabriel d'Orsay, descended from mixed French, German, Italian and Flemish ancestors and 'the Dandy of the Dandies.' He rode in the Park on 'a sensational bay hack, pawing the air.' The best picture of him comes, in fact, not from Samuel Sidney, but from a woman, Jane Welsh Carlyle, wife of the historian Thomas Carlyle. Writing to her mother about Count d'Orsay, Jane spoke of 'the fantastical finery of his dress: sky-blue satin cravat, yards of gold chain, white French gloves, light drab great-coat lined with velvet of the same colour, invisible inexpressibles [i.e. pantaloons] skin-coloured and fitting like a glove.' But she had to admit that, beneath all the finery, his manners were 'manly and unaffected' and that he was 'a devilish clever fellow.'

Combermere was in the Row, too – seventy years old and still riding like a young man. Sir Stapleton Cotton, Viscount Combermere, was a distinguished soldier who had fought in Flanders, Spain and India. Oddly enough, he was not very popular with Wellington. On one occasion, the Government was sending an expedition to Burma with the object of capturing Rangoon. They asked the Duke who was the best man to send. Wellington immediately answered:

'Send Lord Combermere.'

'But,' said the Cabinet, 'we have always understood that your Grace thought Lord Combermere a fool.'

'So he is a fool,' snapped the Duke, 'But he can take Rangoon.'

Only three or four years older than Combermere, the Iron Duke did not appear such an impressive rider in the Park.

'The Duke of Wellington,' wrote Sidney:

never shared the taste of his companions-in-arms for parade chargers and high-school horsemanship. The thorough-bred chestnut Copenhagen, which carried him so stoutly at Waterloo, was only 15 hands high. His horse was a hunter class of animal, a good walker, ridden in a snaffle bridle, like a huntsman's horse, without a thought of showing off the animal's paces. Before age had bent him, his seat was remarkably upright; lost in thought he passed along, mechanically acknowledging with his upraised finger the many hats raised to salute the Great Duke. As he grew old and infirm, instead of bending forward like most old men, he leant back, and literally hung on by the bridle, generally going down St James's Park to the Horse Guards at a huntsman's shog-trot.

Samuel was struck by the way horses matched their riders in character and appearance. The Prime Minister, Lord Melbourne, 'rode exactly the powerful, useful, easy-paced hacks that might have been expected from his character – luxurious and indifferent to appearances.' Lord Palmerston, another Prime Minister, preferred 'tall blood-horses; if they were up to weight, with the best possible road action, could trot ten miles an hour, and gallop, he did not ask for manners, airs, or graces.' This fits well enough with the picture of the hard-working efficient Minister who always worked at a stand-up desk and of whom an omnibus-driver said, pointing to the grey head in the window they were passing:

''E earns 'is wages; I never come by without seeing 'im 'ard at it.'

The man Florence Nightingale should have married and who was responsible for her going to the Crimea, Sidney Herbert, was 'tall, elegant, with a pale, pensive, aristocratic countenance, simply dressed, without a particle of affectation, always riding on a tall blood-horse of the highest character.'

The worst horseman among the statesmen of the period was Sir Robert Peel. In fact, Samuel thought he was 'certainly, if not the very worst, the most awkward horseman that ever bestrode pigskin. He appeared to have no pleasure in the exercise, and performed his ride as a matter of duty, for the sake of health and companionship with his several more or less illustrious colleagues. Sir Robert was killed by a shying hack purchased for him by an excellent judge of horses, the late Lord Ossington, at Tattersall's.'

Sidney Samuel described many more of these figures from another age, giving unusual glimpses of well-known men in the most reveal-ing and most testing predicaments of mankind – on the back of a horse.

It is interesting to compare his picture of Rotten Row with another given over thirty years later in *All the Year Round*, the magazine of which Charles Dickens was editor. This time the emphasis is not on the great ones of the land, but on boys and girls with their ponies.

Of all the sights in London in the month of June, there are few prettier than Rotten Row at that hour in the morning when grave judges, mer-chants of mighty name in the City, and the hard-worked of Her Majesty's Cabinet and Her Majesty's Opposition begin to ride away to their daily, never-ending duties; while the Park is alive with little mobs of boys and girls galloping, trotting, and walking as little as possible, with papa, mamma, or sister Anne, or mostly with some stout and faithful Ruggles, panting and toiling after his precious charges. How bright they look, how happy with innocent excitement glowing on their rosy faces. No thought of heavy acceptances, or of doubtful parliamentary contests, or of ungrateful Ministers of State, checks their ringing laughter, or their cheerful and childish talk. And then what pluck the little creatures have: and how gravely they imitate their seniors, in handling ponies a little bigger than Southdown rams!... Pony-boy-ship, not horse-man-ship, is the crowning glory of these equestrian islands.

The Ladies' Mile, Rotten Row by Gustave Doré from his 'London', 1872

'Blood will carry anything – at least so Miss Featherweight thinks!' – a cartoon from *Punch* by John Leech

It was indeed a pretty picture, but there are many modern young ladies who would disagree violently with what the author went on to say:

The family pony, ridden at all hours, with and without saddle, along bridle-roads, over the moors, in the hayfield, and through the wood, up hill and down dale, teaches the boy to go alone, to defend himself, to tumble cleverly, and to get up again without making a noise at a bump or two ... With girls it is different. A girl can no more learn to ride gracefully than to dance gracefully, without being carefully taught, from the first lesson to the last.

The writings of the period have a good deal to say about the equestrian education of ladies. J. S. Rarey had caustic comments to make about papa's quality as a teacher:

Little girls who learn their first lessons in riding with papa, who is either absorbed in other business, or himself a novice in the art of horsemanship, get into poky habits, which it is extremely difficult to eradicate when they reach the age when every real woman wishes to be admired.

And elsewhere he gives a striking picture of the correct costume for a fashionable horsewoman:

Many ladies entirely spoil the sit of the skirts by retaining the usual impediments of petticoats. The best-dressed horsewomen wear nothing more than a flannel chemise with long coloured sleeves, under their trousers ... There is a prejudice against ladies wearing long Wellington boots; but it is quite absurd, for they need never be seen, and are a great comfort and protection in riding long distances. They should, for obvious reasons, be large enough for long woollen stockings, and easy to get on and off. It would not look well to see a lady struggling out of a pair of wet boots with the help of a bootjack and a couple of chambermaids.

It was assumed that well-brought-up ladies would modestly ride side-saddle, and it is often believed that it is only in modern times that public opinion has so changed that they may ride astride. In fact, in the Middle Ages, women nearly always rode astride; and not till the end of the fourteenth century did the custom of riding side-saddle become common. In one manuscript of Chaucer's *Canterbury Tales*, showing the pilgrims on the road to Canterbury in about 1390, the Prioress sits demurely sideways, but the sturdy Wife of Bath rides boldly astride.

'An alarming incident in "The Row"' – *Punch* has the last word

A Hundred High Horses

No list of horses could ever be complete or satisfy everyone. This one simply records some of which the author has read and heard. Many of his readers may well do better. Horses already dealt with in the text are omitted. Some of the most famous and best-loved horses in the world will not be found in any stud-book, but are fictional creations. In acknowledgement of their high quality and pedigree, a few of these are included.

Adonis   The splendid white charger of George III (1738–1820). It featured in a very large painting, 18 ft wide, by Sir William Beechey, of the king reviewing the Prince of Wales's Regiment of Light Dragoons. An amusing story of the picture (exhibited at the Royal Academy in 1798) was told by a descendant of Beechey:

'When the sketch for the picture was nearing completion, Queen Charlotte came into Sir William Beechey's painting-room at Windsor and asked why the Prince of Wales was not painted in it. Beechey replied that it was as much as his life was worth, bearing in mind the quarrel between H.M. and the Prince. The Queen then suggested that the Prince on his black horse would make a fine foil to the King on his white charger "Adonis". Beechey was struck by the artistic conception, which he allowed to overcome his scruples, so he painted in the Prince.

'Soon afterwards George III came in with his cheery greeting of "Well! Beechey, how are you?" – then, seeing the canvas, angrily exclaimed: "Hey, what, what what! Beechey, the Prince!, d—n the Prince." The King ordered the canvas to be stripped from its support and thrown out of the window, but fortunately it was rescued by an Equerry.'

'George III reviewing the 10th Light Dragoons', by Sir William Beechey

Ambergris   The tallest horse known to have raced. A bay colt, foaled in 1873, it stood 18 hands (6 ft).

Arcibis   Horse belonging to King Menuas, a ruler of ancient Urartu, the Assyrian name for the country later called Armenia. Arcibis, whose name is recorded in an inscription dating from the 8th century B.C., could jump 22 cubits horizontally. A cubit varied in length from about $17\frac{1}{2}$ to 22 inches.

Arundel   The horse of Bevis of Southampton, the legendary hero whose exploits are recounted by the poet Michael Drayton in his long poem 'Poly-Olbion', 1622. Arundel, from the French *hirondelle*, means 'swift as a swallow'.

Asil   Winner of a unique race in 1884, when the field consisted entirely of Arab horses. The next year Asil was beaten by 20 lengths by 'a very moderate horse', thus demonstrating that the Arab has very little chance against the modern thoroughbred racehorse.

Babieca   (meaning 'simpleton'). The favourite horse of the great Castilean hero The Cid, or Cid Campeador – 'the lord champion,' the name given to Rodrigo, Diaz de Bivar (1040–99). As a young man, he ignored all the fine horses he was offered and chose a rough-looking colt. His god-father thereupon called him a simpleton, and the Cid transferred the name to his horse.

El Cid and Babieca

Baly   A great roan draught-horse owned by the brewers Barclay, Perkins & Co. in the 1860s and 1870s. He stood 18 hands and weighed 30 cwt. He was greatly admired by Garibaldi, the Italian revolutionary, during a visit to London in 1864, and was re-named Garibaldi.

Baron of Buchlyvie   A Clydesdale stallion for which the record price for a farm-horse of £9500 was paid at Ayr, Scotland, in 1911.

Bevis   According to Sir Walter Scott, the horse of Lord Marmion, the central character in 'Marmion, A Tale of Flodden Field' set in

Lord Marmion on Bevis from Sir Walter Scott's novel

the year 1513, when James IV of Scotland and his chivalry were disastrously defeated at Flodden. Though Scott's Marmion was fictitious, there were, in fact, several real knights of the name, originating from the lords of Fontenay le Marmion in Normandy.

Biche   A favourite horse of the poet Lord Byron (1788–1824) when he was travelling on the Continent. 'She is young, and as quiet as any of her sex can be – very good tempered, and perpetually neighing when she wants anything, which is every five minutes. I have called her Biche, because her manners are not unlike a little dog's; but she is a very tame, pretty, childish quadruped.'

Big Racket   Officially, the fastest timed horse – 43.26 m.p.h. over a distance of a quarter of a mile, at Lomas de Sotelo, Mexico, 1945.

Black Agnes   The original 'Black Agnes', so called from her dark skin, was Agnes, Countess of Dunbar (*c.* 1312–69), who vigorously defended the castle of Dunbar against Edward III when her husband rebelled against him. She was a lady of courage and high spirit, a daughter of the Earl of Moray. A little over 200 years later, another Earl of Moray, half-brother to Mary, Queen of Scots, gave the queen a black palfrey which he called Black Agnes, presumably as a compliment to his ancestress.

Black Beauty   'I am writing the life of a horse,' wrote Anna Sewell in her journal on 6 November 1871. It was another six years, however, before she published *Black Beauty*, one of the most famous horse stories of all time. Said one admirer: '*Black Beauty* is read by the squire, his lady, their stablemen and boys; and it has taught them to love and care for horses more than any book ever published.' Black Beauty was not 'of the regular tall, carriage-horse breed' but 'had more of the racing blood', standing 'about fifteen and a half hands high and . . . therefore just as good for riding as for driving.'

Black Jack   An English charger taken prisoner at Roleia, Portugal, in 1808, when his master, Colonel Lake, was killed at the head of the 29th Grenadiers. Black Jack became the property of a French general, from whom the horse was bought back by another English officer, Colonel Way, who afterwards rode him in the battles of Douro, Busaco, Talavera and Albuera. On retirement Black Jack became the inseparable friend of an enemy horse. See *Suwarrow*.

Black Saladin   A warhorse of Warwick 'the Kingmaker' – Richard Neville, Earl of Warwick (1428–71), according to one chronicler the 'moost corageous and manliest knight lyving.' See also *Malech*.

Blink Bonny   A famous Yorkshire filly who, in 1857, won the Derby and the Oaks in the same week at Epsom.

Blink Bonny, painted by Harry Hall

Brigadier Gerard   A bay, foaled in 1968, who won 17 out of his 18 races. The Brigadier, 'bred, owned, trained and ridden by Englishmen', was especially noteworthy in an age when American bloodstock was supreme. See *Rataplan*.

Brooklyn Supreme   The heaviest horse recorded – a thorough-bred Belgian stallion, standing nearly 20 hands and weighing over 1 ton 8½ cwt. He came from Iowa, USA. For Belgian, see p. 80.

Bull (or Bulle) Rock   The first thoroughbred horse known to have been brought to America from England, in about 1730. He was foaled in 1718, a son of the Darley Arabian. See p. 62–3.

Carman   The favourite horse of the most famous of European knights – Pierre du Terrail, Seigneur de Bayard, generally known simply as Bayard and as the knight *sans peur et sans reproche* (without fear and without blame). Carman, a fine Persian from the Kerman or Carman district, was given him by the Duke of Lorraine.

Champion Crabbet   Holder of the record for distance and speed, covering 300 miles in 52½ hours, carrying 17½ stone, in 1920.

Citation   A famous Triple Crown winner (the Kentucky Derby, the Preakness and the Belmont Stakes) in America a quarter of a century ago – the first to achieve this and the only one till Secretariat.

Clinker   The favourite horse of Lord Willoughby de Eresby and the cause of a curious incident in 1858. By a strange custom, whose origins are not known, every peer passing through the town of Oakham, Rutland, had to present a horse-shoe to be nailed on the castle gate. Afterwards, the shoes were transferred to the Hall of the castle. The earliest now date from the beginning of the seventeenth century, but the custom is of longer standing than that and may date back to the time when William the Conqueror's farrier, founder of the Ferrers family, lived in or near Oakham.

In 1858, Lord Willoughby de Eresby yielded up a shoe from Clinker which was gilded as a number of others are in the collection. A thief removed it, apparently thinking it was truly made of gold. The shoe was afterwards returned in a parcel to Oakham railway station.

Cole Arabian   A horse belonging to the Prince Regent (later George IV), 'apparently a small animal' yet 'in reality one of the strongest and largest horses of his compass ever seen, shewing at the same time the highest blood possible, with excellent legs and well fixed to the body.' The Prince Regent had a well-known stud at Hampton Court and fancied himself as a horseman, sometimes inventing wild stories about his own proficiency. On one occasion he was with the Duke of Wellington at Devil's Dyke, the valley with almost vertical sides in the Downs just outside Brighton. George IV said to the Duke: 'I galloped down that hill at the head of my regiment.' Without a flicker of surprise on his face, the Duke replied: 'Very steep, sir.'

As a matter of fact, the descent of Devil's Dyke *was* accomplished by one intrepid rider, on 10 October 1815. Mr Poole of Hadgrove, Sussex – 'not only one of the most daring, but one of the best riders in the country' – rode down the steepest part, a distance of some three hundred yards, in the presence of about a hundred sportsmen. He was allowed to diverge only ten yards to left or right of the starting point, but did, in fact, ride almost straight down, not deviating more than three feet. 'He rode an aged mare of his own, who rapidly executed her task, galloping with her fore-feet, and sliding upon her hocks, no less to the astonishment than gratification of all present.'

Copper Bottom   A notable horse in the history of the saddle-horse in America, imported into Kentucky from Canada. The Canadians had crossed mares of French descent with stallions from New York and New England, and produced horses with a fast ambling gait and considerable speed in harness.

Copper Bottom

'Cypron and her brood', by Gilpin

Cypron   The dam of Herod, whose name, in the Herod Line, is given to one of the three outstanding families of British race-horses.

Darius's Horse   Unknown by name, but the winner of a kingdom. Several competitors for the throne of Persia, *c.* 521 B.C., agreed that when they gathered at an agreed meeting place, the claimant whose horse neighed first should have the throne. Darius (after-wards 'the Great') had a groom who took his charger to the place the day before and introduced him to an agreeable mare. Immediately the horses and riders assembled at the appointed spot, Darius's horse gave an appreciative neigh and won his master the throne.

Denmark   A famous 'four-mile' race-horse, son of an English-bred horse taken to the U.S. in the early part of the nineteenth century. It was used to improve the breed of the American saddle-horse, especially the so-called Kentucky saddler, known for its five 'gaits',

i.e. a flat-footed walk, a running walk, the trot, canter and rack—
the last being a fast amble.

Doctor le Gear   The tallest horse recorded, a dapple Percheron
foaled in America in 1902 and standing 7 ft tall (21 hands). The
nose-to-tail measurement was 16 ft. See p. 81 for this breed.

Doctor Syntax   The only horse to win the same race seven years
running. This was the Preston Gold Cup, from 1815–21 inclu-
sive. Doctor Syntax, a pious and simple-minded clergyman, fond
of travelling to escape from his nagging wife, was a character
invented by the writer William Combe (1741–1823).

Doctor Syntax, painted by J. F. Herring

Dodgem   An endearing horse described by Ethelind Fearson in
the autobiographical book *Most Happy Husbandman*. Dodgem,
bought from a circus, was 'the same size and shape as four-and-a-

half gallons of beer', plain brown on one side and skewbald on the other, so that he looked like two different ponies, according to whether he was viewed from the near side or the off.

Dungannon   A son of Eclipse and himself a famous sire at the end of the eighteenth century. Pictures of Dungannon often show him

Dungannon and friend, from a painting by George Stubbs

'Mr Wildman and his sons with Eclipse', by George Stubbs

with a sheep. A drover with a flock, one of which was too exhausted to go farther, left the sheep in Dungannon's meadow. The two became so inseparable that the sheep was purchased as a companion.

Eclipse   One of the most famous race-horses in history, the origin of the saying still heard sometimes today: 'Eclipse first and the rest nowhere.' Eclipse, founder of the Eclipse Line, was foaled in 1764, bred by one of George III's sons, the Duke of Cumberland. Eclipse won or 'walked over' 26 races, eleven of them for the famous King's Plate. He was never beaten and, in 23 years at stud, sired 344 winners. 'Eclipse first . . .' dates from 1769. It is probably the only saying about a race-horse to be recorded in the *Oxford Dictionary of Quotations*.

Eleanor   A thoroughbred mare owned by Sir Charles Bunbury. He made a wager that the mare could carry a greater weight than

Eleanor

a strong working horse. The selected opponent was a miller's horse, accustomed to carrying heavy loads of corn and meal. Eleanor walked away under an enormous load beneath which the miller's horse could scarcely stand, let alone go forward. She also accomplished the rare feat of winning both the Oaks and the Derby in 1801.

Emir   Credited with winning the longest race in history – 1200 miles, in Portugal.

Fadda   The white mule of Mahomet (Muhammed, Mohammed), *c.* 570–632, the founder of the religious and social system named after him.

Fisherman   Holder of the record for winning the most races in a single season – 23 in 1856.

Flatfoot   A horse ridden by Mr Elliott, 'of the Bedchamber', against Charles II at Newmarket in October 1671. The king was beaten, but did better two days later, winning a handsome flagon.

Flora   A horse belonging to Lord Darlington (1766–1842) which executed a famous leap over a hedge four feet high and across the ditch behind, the ditch being seven and three-quarter yards wide from the top of the hedge. Flora was described as 'a hunting mare of the Old English breed.' See also *Philippic*.

Flying Childers   Had the reputation of being the fastest horse that ever ran at Newmarket and, indeed, that was ever born. He was bred in 1715 by the Duke of Devonshire and is recorded as having run four miles in six minutes forty-eight seconds ($35\frac{1}{2}$ m.p.h.) carrying nine stone two pounds. If this is true, it is an all-time record, since the best official three-mile time is 5 minutes 15 seconds at 34.29 m.p.h. (1941).

Flying Childers (right), engraved from a painting by J. N. Sartorius

Formosa, drawn in 1868 by Harry Hall

Formosa   A sensation in the year 1868, winning the four so-called English 'classics' – the Oaks, the St Leger, the 1000 Guineas and the 2000 Guineas. Formosa nearly became the only horse in history to win all five classics (the fifth being the Derby), but ran a dead heat.

Gyalpo   The horse used by the intrepid woman traveller Isabella Lucy Bishop (*née* Bird) on a journey through India to Tibet. Mrs Bishop (1831–1904) was one of the greatest travellers of her time, most of her expeditions being accomplished alone. During her journey to Tibet, at altitudes of up to 17,000 ft, she wrote: 'I wish I could send my Badakshan horse Gyalpo to Lord Middleton's stud to be the sire of a race of horses. He goes anywhere and does anything – even over the Kharzing Glacier last week, and swam the rapids of the Shayok; not an old woman's horse, but I contrive to get on with him.'

Mrs Bishop was the first woman to be elected a Fellow of the Royal Geographical Society.

Hambletonian A famous American horse (also known as Rysdyk's Hambletonian), 'the great modern progenitor of fast trotters'. Foaled in 1849, at Sugar Loaf, Orange County, N.Y., he was bought, with his dam, for $125 by a farm-hand named William Rysdyk. At first his stud fee was only $35, then a number of his progeny and descendants scored brilliant successes and it was

Rysdyk's Hambletonian with his owner, after a painting by James H. Wright in 1865

realized what a great sire Hambletonian was. When he died in 1876 he had begotten about 1333 foals from whom have descended almost every record-breaking trotter in the book. At 25 years old, Hambletonian stood $15\frac{1}{4}$ hands high at the withers. Oddly enough, though all his fastest progeny were short, he was long in the body, with great muscular power.

Herod   Horse giving its name to the Herod Line, one of the three chief families in the history of the British race-horse. Herod was the great-great-grandson of the Byerley Turk. (See p. 61–2).

King Herod, known as Herod. Courtesy of Fores Ltd

Incitatus   The favourite horse – his name means 'spurred on' – of the Roman emperor Gaius Caesar Germanicus (A.D. 12–41), usually known as Caligula from the *caligae* or soldier's boots he often wore. Incitatus is said to have been given royal honours, an ivory stall in a marble stable and a jewelled collar. He was waited on by slaves, and guests were bidden to feasts in his name.

Jack   The much-loved pony of Robert Louis Stevenson in Samoa, bought in 1890. Jack was so temperamental that even the sight of a bunch of bananas in the road would cause him to sit down in fright. He was 'a *very* plain animal, dark brown, but a good goer, and gentle, except for a habit of shying and sitting down on his tail.'

Jenny Geddes   A mare ridden by the poet Robert Burns (1759–1796). In 1637, with the support of Charles I, Archbishop Laud attempted to introduce a new service book into Scotland. There was great resistance and, when Bishop James Lindsay (who had crowned Charles I at Holyrood) climbed into the pulpit in St Giles Cathedral, Edinburgh, a member of the congregation, whose name is reported to have been Jenny Geddes, threw a stool at him. Many thought that Jenny was a man in disguise; others maintain that, in that case, the stool would have hit the bishop instead of going wide.

Robert Burns on Jenny Geddes

John Gilpin's ride, by T. Stothard

John Gilpin's Horse One of the most famous horses in English literature though the poet concerned, William Cowper (1731–1800), did not give it a name in the celebrated ballad of John Gilpin's ride. Gilpin is described as a linen-draper and train-band captain. After twenty years of marriage without a holiday, his wife suggested they should take the day off and dine as a family party at the Bell in Edmonton. Mrs Gilpin, their four children and her sister, went ahead by chaise, Gilpin promising to follow on horseback. He borrowed the horse from his friend 'the calender', i.e. a man engaged in the trade of giving cloth and paper a smooth, glossy appearance by using rollers, etc. All we know of the mount was that he had a flowing mane and was 'nimble'. He was also probably under-exercised for, when he left the city streets, he took to his heels in fine style, flying right past the inn in Edmonton and not stopping till he reached Ware, the home of his owner, the calender. Here Gilpin turned the horse round and galloped back, faring no better than before, for he was again carried past the inn, cheered on as before by the crowds, who thought he was riding a race.

The poem is a thoroughly amusing, rollicking affair, not at all typical of Cowper, who suffered from acute bouts of melancholy. It was to relieve one of these bouts that his friend Lady Austin told him the story, which that same night, in 1782, he turned into verse.

Kincsem   A famous Hungarian mare, born in 1874 which, over the years 1877–1880, was unbeaten in 54 races.

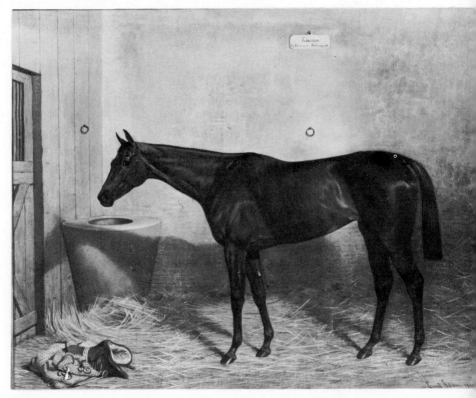

Kincsem, painted by Emil Adam in 1895

La Fleche   Winner of four classics in one year (1892), the Oaks, the St Leger, the Cambridgeshire and the 1000 Guineas.

Lamri   In literature, King Arthur's mare. The name means 'the curveter.' A curvet is a special kind of leap in which the horse raises both fore-legs at once and, as they are falling, raises his hind legs, so that all four legs are in the air at the same time. The term is

King Arthur, mounted on Lamri, discovering the skeletons of his brothers, by Gustave Doré

Lexington

often found, however, in poetry and stories, for any sort of frolic-some leaping.

Lexington Probably the most famous thoroughbred ever raised in America. Foaled in 1850, his blood 'is everywhere throughout the fabric of the American race-horse.' Lexington, in Kentucky, is a famous horse-breeding centre. One of its most notable features is the 1873 Trotting Track, with its mile oval where most of the world's trotting and pacing records have been established.

Mahmoud Holder of the record time for the Derby, running the race in 2 minutes 33.8 seconds (i.e. an average speed of over 35 m.p.h.) in 1936. Mahmoud is one of the horses—Le Sancy was

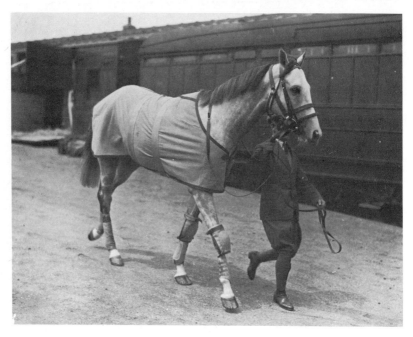

Mahmoud, the Aga Khan's famous race-horse

another—that for ever killed the long-held belief that no grey can be a fast horse, compared with bay, chestnut, etc.

Malech   Sire of Black Saladin, the coal-black charger of Warwick 'the Kingmaker' (1428–71). According to tradition, when the line of Malech failed, the race of Warwick would end also. Warwick was killed at the Battle of Barnet, 14 April 1471, leaving only two daughters.

Maltese Cat   'Past Pluperfect Player of the Game' of polo, in one of Kipling's Indian stories. At the end of the day when the Cup had been won, 'a wise little, plain little, head looked in through the open door' and 'he limped in to the blaze of light and the glittering uniforms ... was petted all round the table, moving gingerly;

and they drank his health because he had done more to win the Cup than any man or horse on the ground.'

Man o' War   Famous American horse, foaled 1917, raced 1919–20, considered 'one of the supreme thoroughbreds of history.'

Mare Swallow   According to Charles Kingsley (1819–75), the horse belonging to the English outlaw Hereward the Wake whose dates are uncertain but who was active in the 1070s, in the reign of William I. Mare Swallow was 'the ugliest as well as the swiftest of mares' with a 'great chuckle-head, greyhound flanks, and drooping hind quarters.'

Man O'War, the Kentucky 'Wonder Horse', in 1917 with Clarence Kummer up

Marshland Shales   A famous one-eyed horse encountered by George Borrow (1803–81) during his travels. With 'nothing very remarkable' about him to distinguish him from his fellows, Borrow was amazed to see men taking off their hats to him and greeting him with every mark of respect.

'The best in mother England,' explained one old man .... 'He is old like myself, but can still trot his twenty miles a day ... If you should chance to reach my years, you may boast to thy great grand boys, thou hast seen Marshland Shales.'

Borrow did what he 'would neither do for earl nor baron', and took off his hat with the rest.

Matchem   Horse giving his name to the Matchem Line, one of the outstanding families in British racing history. Matchem's grand-sire was the famous Godolphin Arab, and his dam descended from the Byerley Turk. (See pp. 61–3).

Matchem, by John Wootton

The story of Mazeppa, engraved from a painting by J. F. Herring

Mazeppa   One of Astley's best-known horses. (See pp. 47–50.) He was undoubtedly named after Mazeppa, a page at the court of Jan Casimir of Poland (reigned 1648–68). Mazeppa had a love affair with the wife of a young Polish count who had the page tied naked to the back of a wild horse and sent off into the barren steppes. The story seems to have some basis in historical fact. Mazeppa – his name is properly Ivan Stepanovich Mazepa-Koledinsky – was rescued by Cossacks and became one of their greatest leaders. The story of Mazeppa's ride is told in a poem by Lord Byron and is the subject of several paintings.

In truth he was a noble steed,   *In the full foam of wrath and dread*
A Tartar of the Ukraine breed . . .   *To me the desert-born was led.*

Messenger   Founder of a famous line of 'trotters' or trotting horses in the U.S.A. about a century ago. He probably sired about 1000 horses. In trotting, the horse makes simultaneous use of diagonally opposite legs, whereas in pacing the horse moves fore and hind legs simultaneously on one side.

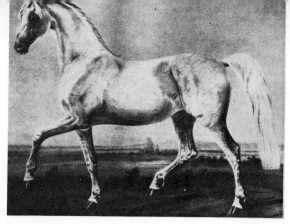

Messenger, from the Hall of Fame of the Trotter, U.S.A.

Mill Reef A bay colt, born 1968. Bred in America, he was trained in England and won 12 of the 14 races he ran in, winning the record sum in Europe of £300,422. A broken leg ended his career on the course, robbing him of a second encounter against Brigadier Gerard (see above), one of the only horses to beat him.

Mill Reef an easy winner of the 1971 Prix de l'Arc de Triomphe at Longchamps in France

Molly The horse, which lived 35 years, of the great soldier Sir Charles Napier (1782–1853) who made his reputation in India, both as commander and administrator. One of the best anecdotes about him concerns his annexation of the territory of Sind, in the lower valley of the Indus. Though he had no moral right to seize it, he believed he was politically justified and afterwards sent a dispatch consisting of the single Latin word *Peccavi*, which means 'I have sinned (Sind).'

Old Marske Sire of the great Eclipse (see above).

Oscar A 'glorious high-caste Arab' owned by a well-known soldier, Lieut.-Col. B. D. Wardlaw Ramsay, in India. He would bear
nothing but a plain light snaffle and was otherwise vicious and un-
controllable. Once, when Ramsay rode him with a crupper at a
review, Oscar 'kicked the crupper to bits and then, annoyed by
the firing of the guns, took the bit in his teeth, galloped right up to
them, and took hold of one of the guns, actually screaming with
rage.'

Pegasus on a
Carthaginian
decadrachm,
4th Century BC
(*left*) and (*right*)
on a Corinthian
stator, 4th
Century BC

Pegasus In mythology, the winged horse which was ridden by
Bellerophon, hero of many exploits. According to the Greek poet
Hesiod, Pegasus was so named because he was born at the springs
(*pegoe*) of Ocean. On his birth he soared into the air and made his
first landing where the acropolis at Corinth stands. While he was
drinking at the fountain, Bellerophon caught and tamed him. The
winged Pegasus appears on many of the early coins of Corinth.

Philippic A hunter ridden by Lord Carmarthen, son of the Duke
of Leeds, which made a memorable leap in 1815, in the neigh-
bourhood of Hornby Castle, Yorkshire. Lord Carmarthen put the

145

horse at a brook full to the banks and cleared it. The leap from hind foot to front fore foot was measured at 26 feet 9 ins. This can be compared with the biggest jump on the Grand National Course (the 15th, known as the Open Ditch), which has a hedge beyond it 5 feet 2 inches high and 3 feet 9 ins wide. The ditch on the take off side is 6 feet wide.

Prejevalski's rare Mongolian Wild Horse

Pretty Polly, by J. Beer

Prejevalski's Horse   The wild horse named after the Russian explorer to whom it was presented in 1879, the first specimen known in modern Europe. In 1902 an expedition to the Gobi region, led by Karl Hagenbeck of Hamburg and helped by 2000 Kirghis tribesmen, captured 32 foals, from which many specimens have been bred and distributed in various zoological gardens. An average specimen is about 4 feet (12 hands) high.

Pretty Polly   Winner of the Oaks, the St Leger and the 1000 Guineas in 1904.

Rataplan   The black charger of Brigadier Étienne Gérard, the boastful but lovable hero of several books by Sir Arthur Conan

Doyle. Gerard, according to himself, was the finest horseman and surest blade in the ten regiments of Hussars. Another of his mounts was the little grey mare Violette, 'the fastest horse in the six brigades of light cavalry.' The Brigadier would have considered it only his due to have a famous twentieth-century horse named after him. (See this list).

Roan Barbary According to Shakespeare, the favourite charger of Richard II, which would eat from his master's hand but which, when Richard resigned the crown, carried his triumphant successor (Henry IV, often called Henry of Bolingbroke) instead.

Oh, how it yearned my heart, when I beheld
In London streets that coronation day,
When Bolingbroke rode on Roan Barbary!

Roland The horse that carried the hero of Browning's spirited poem *How they brought the Good News from Ghent to Aix*, published in 1845. It is a thrilling, but imaginary, story of three horsemen

'Till at length into Aix Roland galloped', from Browning's poem

galloping without rest, 'from moonset to sunrise, from sunrise into the blaze of noon.' Only Roland, urged on by his desperate rider, finally reached Aix, to be given a suitable welcome by the citizens.

And all I remember is, friends flocking round
As I sate with his head 'twixt my knees on the ground,
And no voice but was praising this Roland of mine,
As I poured down his throat our last measure of wine.
Which (the burgesses voted by common consent)
Was no more than his due who brought good news from Ghent.

Ronald   The chestnut horse ridden by Lord Cardigan at the Battle of Balaclava (1854), when he led the famous charge of the Light Cavalry Brigade. Ronald had four white legs and so proved false the old Devonshire rhyme:

If you have a horse with four white legs,
  Keep him not a day;
If you have a horse with three white legs,
  Send him far away;
If you have a horse with two white legs,
  Sell him to a friend;
If you have a horse with one white leg,
  Keep him to the end.

Rosabelle   The favourite palfrey of Mary Queen of Scots (1542–1587). A palfrey was a small saddle-horse of good breeding, especially suitable for ladies. Its pleasant disposition and ease of control also made it popular for ceremonial and parade purposes. The Monk in Chaucer's *Canterbury Tales*, who had many horses in his stable, chose a palfrey 'broun as a berye' to ride on his pilgrimage to Canterbury.

Rosinante   The horse of Don Quixote de la Mancha, the would-be knight of Miguel de Cervantes' famous satire on the chivalric romances of the Middle Ages. Rosinante, in keeping with her

'It was yet early in the morning, at which time the sunbeams did not prove so offensive.' An engraving of Cervantes' Don Quixote and his companion Sancho Panza by Gustave Doré

master's curious appearance, was all skin and bone. The name comes from the Spanish *rocin-ante*, meaning formerly a hack or jade, i.e. the most worthless type of horse, far removed from the knightly charger or destrier.

Saltmarsh Silver Crest The heaviest horse so far known in Britain, a Percheron stallion born in 1956 and weighing 1 ton 4.75 cwt (2772 lb).

Sceptre at Newmarket, 1911

Savoy A black charger belonging to Charles VIII of France (1470–1498). It was named after the Duke of Savoy, who presented it to Charles, though it was 'mean in stature' and had only one eye.

Sceptre The horse who so far this century has come nearest to achieving the feat of winning the five classics in a single season. In 1902, Sceptre won the 1000 Guineas, the 2000 Guineas, the Oaks and the St Leger.

Seabird An unusual horse in that he was a rather poor two-year-old but was superb as a three-year-old. Born in 1962, he won seven of his eight races, including the Epsom Derby and the Prix de l'Arc de Triomphe (1965). In the latter, which he won by 6 lengths, the field included five Derby winners.

A happy moment after Seabird's triumph in the Epsom Derby in 1965

Secretariat at full stretch – a bronze by John Skeaping

Secretariat The greatest American horse of recent years and one of the most valuable on record, bought by a syndicate for $6,080,000 and sent to stud in 1973. He had previously won the Triple Crown, i.e. the Kentucky Derby, the Preakness and the Belmont Stakes.

Signoretta An Italian horse, owned by the Chevalier Ginistrelli, which, in 1908, 'astonished the world' by winning the Derby at the long odds of 100-1 and the Oaks two days later.

Sleipnir In Scandinavian mythology, the grey horse of Odin, chief of the gods. Sleipnir had eight legs and could travel by sea and land.

Sorrel One of the horses that changed the course of history. Riding him in Hampton Court Park in 1702, William III of England was badly thrown when the horse stumbled over a mole-hill. The king was too frail to recover. Supporters of the exiled Stuarts (the Jacobites) used to drink toasts to 'the little gentleman in black velvet', i.e. the mole that caused the fatal spill and, they hoped, brought nearer the return of the true Stuart line.

The most noble ROBERT
Earle of Essex and Ewe, Earle
Marshall of England, Vicount He-
reford and Bourchier, Lord Ferres
of Chartley, L. Bourcher and
Louayn, and her Maiesties
lieutenant, and Gouernour generall
of the Kingdome of Irland. 1601.

Robert Devereux, the Earl of Essex, engraved by R. Boissard

Soueida Holder of a speed record for the mile – 1 minute 31.8 seconds (39.21 m.p.h.) at Brighton, Sussex, in 1963. A downhill course was a great help.

Suleiman A favourite horse of Robert Devereux, Earl of Essex (1566–1601), favourite of Queen Elizabeth I till his arrogance and alleged treachery led to his trial and execution. The horse was probably named after Suleiman the Magnificent (1494–1566), sultan of the Ottoman Empire.

Suwarrow Once the property of the Grand Vizier of the Turkish empire, and captured in battle. He was then owned by the Russian general Count Aleksandr Vasilyevich Suwarrow (or Suvorov, 1729–1800) and was later brought to England by the Russian ambassador and presented to Lord Sheffield who, in turn, gave him to his nephew Colonel Way. Suwarrow became the inseparable friend of Black Jack (see above) and 'if separated for a moment, they expressed the greatest impatience, by neighing and restlessness.'

Tetrarch The famous 'spotted rocking horse', whom his great jockey, Steve Donoghue, considered the world's fastest horse and 'a freak never likely to be seen again'. He was unbeaten in seven races as a two year old in 1913, but the 1914–18 War brought his remarkable career to an end. He would only run straight out in front at tremendous speed. That and his curious rocking gait made him unique. (See pp. 71–2).

Topolino Credited with being the longest-lived horse in history. He was an Italian horse, born in Libya in 1909, and survived till 1960, aged 51 years.

Traveller The favourite mount of General Robert E. Lee (1807–70), one of the greatest leaders of the southern, or Confederate,

153

states in the American Civil War. Lee said only a poet could properly describe Traveller's 'endurance of toil, hunger, thirst, cold and the dangers of suffering through which he passed.' When

General Robert E. Lee mounted on Traveller surrenders to General Grant at Appomattox, 1865, painted by Sidney King

he was asked to describe the horse, Lee replied: 'I am not an artist, and can only say he is a Confederate Gray' – a reference to the grey field uniforms worn by the southern troops.

Trigger   A white horse, probably an Arabian, rescued from an old-iron man by William Holt, who journeyed with him all over the world, sleeping rough and sharing everything together. The pair became the subject of several books.

Violette   See *Rataplan*.

William Holt and Trigger
enjoy a treat in Rome

Field-Marshall Earl Roberts on his charger, Vonolel, painted by C. W. Furse

Vonolel   The favourite charger of Field-Marshal Lord Roberts, known as 'Bobs' (1832–1914), who fought in the Indian Mutiny and the South African War.

Wandle Robert   The tallest horse known to have been bred in Britain – a Shire stallion owned by the brewing firm of Young & Co. and standing 6 feet $1\frac{1}{2}$ inches (18.3 hands). See p. 82 for the breed.

Wandle Robert

Warrior   The famous horse of General Jack Seely (later Lord Mottistone, 1868–1947) who commanded a Canadian Cavalry Brigade in France, 1914–18. Seely, who afterwards wrote Warrior's biography, always maintained that the horse was responsible for the capture of the Moreuil Ridge and thus saved Amiens.

White Horse, The   Symbol of power used by some of the Saxon kings and chiefs. It was on the standard of the chieftains who invaded Kent, *c.* 449, and it is still the badge of the County of Kent. Cut in the chalk downs of Berkshire is a 374-foot-long white horse, marking the victory of Alfred over the Danes in 871. (See p. 76).

White Surrey   Horse associated by Shakespeare with Richard III of England.

Fill me a bowl of wine. Give me a watch.
Saddle white Surrey for the field tomorrow.

The 'field' was the Battle of Bosworth, 1485, when Richard III was killed and the Tudor line came to the throne.

Winnie   The young strawberry blood-mare belonging to Tom Faggus the highwayman in R. D. Blackmore's famous novel *Lorna Doone*. She was 'wonderfully beautiful, with her supple stride, and soft slope of shoulder, and glossy coat beaded with water, and prominent eyes, full of love or of fire.' John Ridd, who boasted that 'there was never horse upon Exmoor foaled, but I could tackle in half-an-hour' without saddle, was given the chance to ride her by Tom Faggus. The story of the subsequent ride is worth the reading.

An illustration from R. D. Blackmore's *Lorna Doone*

156

Woodcock   A race-horse successfully ridden by Charles II of England at Newmarket.

Wooden Horse of Troy   The famous horse, described by the poet Virgil, built by Ulysses under the walls of Troy. The Trojans obligingly dragged the monster within their walls, only to find that it was full of Greek soldiers, who stole out at night and opened the gates before setting fire to the city.

The wooden horse of Troy, painted by Tiepolo

Zad-er-Rakib   One of the earliest named horses known to history. It is recorded by an Arab historian as belonging to King Solomon (*c.* 986–932 B.C.).